Out of the Frying Pan

A Comedy in Three Acts

by Francis Swann

A SAMUEL FRENCH ACTING EDITION

SAMUEL FRENCH

FOUNDED 1830

New York Hollywood London Toronto

SAMUELFRENCH.COM

OUT OF THE FRYING PAN

STORY OF THE PLAY

Produced with notable success at the Windsor Theatre in New York City by William Deering and Alexander Kirkland. Three young men and three young women are sharing an apartment. They are would-be stage folk and they have been driven to this community scheme by the lack of economic security. It is a whacky plan they have in mind, for the apartment they rent is immediately above that of a Broadway producer who has quite a hit running and is about to cast a road company. They rehearse the play which he is currently producing, but the problem is—how to get him upstairs to see it? The plans are further complicated by the fact that a snippy young friend of one of the girls enters the picture and threatens to tell the girl's father that she is living in what could most politely be called an unusual manner. Now, it so happens that the producer is an amateur chef of some considerable ability, and right in the middle of a culinary concoction he runs out of flour. He comes upstairs to borrow a cup. At last! The kids have him in the house, and they aren't going to let him out until he sees some evidence of their ability. So to impress him they stage a murder scene. It is so realistic that police swarm into the scene and the misunderstanding becomes hilarious when it is discovered the girl who is

STORY OF THE PLAY

playing the corpse has been served a Mickey Finn. However, in spite of everything, what seems to be a profitable friendship springs up, and Equity dues get paid and the landlady gets the back rent, and it looks as if the future might hold some promise for the youngsters. Highly recommended. "—a gay bit of nonsense that makes an agreeable evening in the theatre."—Sidney B. Whipple, *New York World-Telegram.* "—proved to be one of the merriest Broadway events in weeks—it has an underlying ring of truth that makes it human as well as amusing."—*New York Post.* "It kept an appreciative audience laughing almost continuously both for its sheer artlessness and humorous situations."—*New York Journal and American.*

Copy of program of the first performance of OUT
OF THE FRYING PAN as produced at the Windsor Theatre, New York:

William Deering and Alexander Kirkland

present

"OUT OF THE FRYING PAN"

A new comedy by Francis Swann

Staged by Mr. Kirkland

CAST
(In order of appearance)

GEORGE BODELL .... *William W. Terry*
NORMAN REESE .... *Alfred Drake*
MRS. GARNET .... *Mabel Paige*
TONY DENNISON .... *Sellwyn Myers*
MURIEL FOSTER .... *Florence MacMichael*
KATE AULT .... *Nancy Douglass*
MARGE BENSON .... *Louise Snyder*
DOTTIE COBURN .... *Barbara Bell Geddes*
MR. COBURN .... *Henry Antrim*
MR. KENNY .... *Reynolds Evans*
MAC .... *Arthur Holland*
JOE .... *George Mathews*

The entire action of the play takes place in the living room of a brownstone front apartment in New York City.

ACT ONE

SCENE 1: *Late Friday afternoon in October.*

SCENE 2: *Saturday morning.*

ACT TWO

Saturday evening.

ACT THREE

Sunday morning.

The characters and events in this play are purely imaginary, and anyone claiming resemblance or similarity ought to be ashamed to admit it.

DESCRIPTION OF CHARACTERS

GEORGE BODELL: *About 23. A large, lazy and completely good-natured young man. His voice is slow, and he has a dry, flat way of saying things.*

NORMAN REESE: *Aged 22. He is the capable member of the group. He takes care of things, sees that appointments are kept, watches over the others like a mother hen with her chicks.*

TONY DENNISON: *The handsomest of the three boys. He is tall and deeply sincere, but is inclined to be a bit discouraged at the moment. About 24.*

KATE AULT: *Kate is the cynic of the crowd. She is tall and dark. She has probably been in New York trying to get a "break" in the theater for a longer time than any of the others. About 21.*

MARGE BENSON: *Young, dark and attractive—a little more serious than the others—and in being more serious, seems a little older—about 21.*

DOTTIE COBURN: *A petite, blonde girl, young and attractive, always a little vague. She is of the "Dumb Dora" type, but quite cheerful and happy about everything. She is the baby of the crowd—aged 18—but seems to be even younger than that.*

NOTE: *It is quite important that the six kids be shown as likable, attractive, normal young boys and girls. They are not at all like the popular conception of actors and actresses living in New York. They are healthy American kids, from all parts of the country.*

MRS. GARNET: *Who is their bewildered and uncomplaining landlady. She is never quite sure whether she is watching a play or a scene from real life. Probably the answer to it all is that behind her whimsical exterior she is envious, because she is stage struck, too.*

MURIEL FOSTER: *Dottie's friend from Boston. She is petulant, suspicious, and later on, woe-begone, with a voice like a tired Minnie Mouse. In spite of all this, she is not unattractive. Dottie's age.*

ARTHUR KENNY: *Middle-aged, with a sharp jaw and a dry, unemotional voice that accompanies an habitual sphinx-like expression. He is dignified at all times, fastidious and dresses well.*

MR. COBURN: *A successful business man turned politician. He is on the Board of Censors in Boston—of some wealth, just enough to be snobbish. He explodes rather easily, but tries to maintain his dignity.*

FIRST COP: *The intellectual type of policeman—a career man. He tries very hard and wants to be obliging.*

SECOND COP: *The dumb but earnest type. Even if you drew him a diagram he would not understand it.*

Copy of program of the first production of OUT OF
THE FRYING PAN as produced at The Hilltop
Theatre, Ellicott City, Md., under management
of Don Swann, Jr.:

The Hilltop Theatre
presents
The World Premiere

"OUT OF THE FRYING PAN"

By FRANCIS SWANN

Directed by the Author

GEORGE BODELL .... *Alexander Armstrong, Jr.*
MRS. GARNET .... *Clara Cedrone*
NORMAN REESE .... *Allan Dale, Jr.*
MURIEL FOSTER .... *Florence MacMichael*
KATE AULT .... *Lyn Swann*
MARGE BENSON .... *Jean Price*
TONY FOSTER .... *Richard Cowdery*
DOTTIE COBURN .... *Mary Jane Stockham*
LADY .... *Caroline Woods*
MR. COBURN .... *W. Ramont Hamel*
MRS. COBURN .... *Jane Sauer*
MR. KENNETT .... *Thad Sharretts*
FIRST POLICEMAN .... *Pinkney McLean*
SECOND POLICEMAN .... *Irving Baum*

Settings designed by Robert Dobson, W. Ramont
Hamel, and Don Swann, Jr.

Stage manager—Jane Sauer

*The entire action of the play takes place in the living
room of a studio apartment on a side street off
Fifth Avenue.*

9

TIME: *The present.*

ACT I

SCENE 1—*Late Friday afternoon in November.*
SCENE 2—*Saturday morning.*

INTERMISSION

ACT II

Saturday evening.

INTERMISSION—Singing on the Porticoe.

ACT III

Sunday morning.

Costumes by A. T. Jones and Son.

NOTE: In the New York production the characters of MRS. COBURN and LADY were eliminated.

Out Of The Frying Pan

ACT ONE

Scene I

Scene: *There is an arch rear Center where a one-step bay makes the vestibule. Apartment door (c.) opens onto this at Center. There is a brass knocker on this door. At Right Center (r.c.) in the rear wall is the door to the bathroom, and in the upper Left wall is a two-way swinging door (l.2) to the kitchen. Further down Left wall is the door (l.1) to the girls' bedroom. At Right one of a pair of panelled doors (r.) opens into the front room which is used as the boys' bedroom. Below this door stands a radiator, the pipe of which goes into the floor at the downstage end. A pipe rises right through the room in the corner of the jog and the door Left 1. Below the jog is another radiator, its pipe toward Center. On the right side of Center arch is a small box with downstairs' door buzzer mounted on it. The entire stage is covered with brown carpet. The walls are faded pink and silver stripe. The vestibule is a neutral figure. The picture molding is gold; the woodwork is oyster, except the double doors Right, which are dark. Hanging on the wall between the bath-*

room door and the arch is a bulletin board with notes and a letter; and on the wall, at Left of the arch, is an accordion coat hanger, each hook of which has a label designating its owner. Thumb-tacked to the wall over the radiator Left is a color sheet from the "Daily Mirror" Sunday Drama Section of The Lunts in "There Shall Be No Night," and on the wall at Right of bathroom door is one of Katherine Cornell. Hung on the doorway Right are old red draperies trimmed with tan fringe. On the walls down Right and Left are old two-globed converted lamp brackets.

Below the bulletin board is a fake bookcase. In the corner up Right is a round table and a gilded cafe chair; duplicate chair stands at Left Center. At Right Center is a dilapidated sofa-day-bed, the head end toward up Right. Down Left is an old-fashioned turtle-back trunk with cushions piled upon it. Up Left Center under the hatrack is a piano bench.

Through the door Right can be seen an old grey-painted kitchen chair. On the bathroom backing hangs a towel rack on which can be seen two towels. On the offstage side of door Left 2 hang two pot holders on a hook. Kitchen pots and pans can be seen on the kitchen backing. Through the door Left 1 can be seen a traveling case. On each side of Center arch, at Right of the bathroom door and downstage side of doorway Right are large hooks for the wash lines. Through the Center door a flight of stairs can be seen in the dim hall. There is a telephone bell box on the Right side of the door. The phone on a long cable sits on the bookcase.

On the table is an empty skull humidor; a pipe rack containing three pipes; an empty gold-fish globe; a stuffed owl; a lamp, a knife box

*containing five knives and forks; a Samuel
French edition of "Mostly Murder" is on top
of the bookcase. Have prop books fastened to
shelves. On the step, at the Left, is a pile of
New York phone books. A fencing mask hangs
on the harrack. A fencing foil stands in the
corner Left of bench. Under the bench are
papers—a copy of "Billboard" and one of
"Variety." On the sofa is a bed pillow in which
stands a large knife. On the bathroom door is
a sign reading, "Standing Room Only."*

*It is evening. The wall brackets and lamp are lighted.
The bedroom doors are open.*

*At rise the knife in the pillow is quivering as if just
thrown.* GEORGE *stands at Center, about to throw
a duplicate knife. As he raises it overhead, three
loud, commanding KNOCKS on the entrance
door are heard.* GEORGE *cringes; hides the knife
behind his back; slowly approaches the door
and throws it open.* NORMAN *enters.*

NORMAN. *(Enters. At* GEORGE'S R.*)* Oh—there
you are. What happened to that corpse?

GEORGE. You mean that ratty old corpse, sir? It
disappeared.

NORMAN. *(Advancing)* This is most perplexing.

GEORGE. Quite.

(There is a KNOCK at the C. *door. They pay no
attention.)*

NORMAN. I'm not at all sure that you are entirely
without blame.

*(*MRS. GARNET, *the landlady, enters with a box of
laundry.)*

GEORGE. Why should I want to murder that poor unfortunate girl?

NORMAN. If only I knew that. *(Approaches GEORGE, and with a twist of the wrist, gets the knife away from him—then threatening him with it. GEORGE staggers onto chair L.C.)*

MRS. GARNET. *(Screams at sight of knife)* Oh!

NORMAN. *(To her)* It's all right. *(To GEORGE)* So. Now, then—what do you know about it?

MRS. GARNET. *(Pleasantly)* Excuse me. Is Miss Coburn here?

GEORGE. I don't know anything. I never saw the girl.

MRS. GARNET. It's her laundry. I paid for it.

NORMAN. You were in the room when she was stabbed through the heart!

MRS. GARNET. And there's the rent, too.

NORMAN. Speak up, damn you!

MRS. GARNET. I say—there's the rent, too.

NORMAN. *(To MRS. GARNET)* Please! *(To GEORGE)* Nevertheless, there are strange and weird things occurring tonight in Brooklyn. That peculiar woman—

(MRS. GARNET *puts laundry on foot of sofa.)*

GEORGE. Do not speak of her. She is good and kind and pure. She is my light—my bright angel—

MRS. GARNET. Just the same, this was a dollar eighty-three.

NORMAN. *(To MRS. GARNET)* We're trying to rehearse! *(Goes up R.; puts knife on table.)*

GEORGE. *(Dropping his characterization)* How can we, with all these interruptions? *(He takes a Samuel French edition of "Mostly Murder" from his hip pocket and begins to study.)*

MRS. GARNET. It seems very odd. There were nine men's shirts.

NORMAN. Good. *(Puts pillow on table.)*

MRS. GARNET. I don't understand it. When Miss Coburn took this apartment, she said she might have another girl visiting her from time to time, but—well—nine men's shirts!

NORMAN. I'll speak to Miss Coburn when she comes in.

MRS. GARNET. I wish you would. *(Going to c. door)* The laundry man looked at me so funny. He thought it was my wash—imagine!

NORMAN. I can't.

MRS. GARNET. No. I tried, but it wasn't any use.

GEORGE. *(Reading from manuscript)* "Farewell, bright angel."

MRS. GARNET. *(Doubtfully)* Farewell. *(Exits c.)*

GEORGE. *(Rises)* Norman, I just can't get these lines!

NORMAN. *(Opening laundry)* Don't worry about the lines. If you forget them, improvise!

GEORGE. *(L.C., foot on chair)* Don't start that Stanislavsky business again.

NORMAN. Why not? He knew what he was talking about. Make up a character. Get so thoroughly into the part that whatever you say is right. That's acting!

GEORGE. Sounds like an awful lot of work to me.

NORMAN. No, it isn't. It's like playing a game. Look—pretend you're the Man in the Iron Mask. That ought to hold you for a start.

(GEORGE crosses L. to below radiator. TONY enters c. GEORGE holds his head, trying to imagine an iron mask.)

TONY. What did Mrs. Garnet want?

NORMAN. Money.

TONY. Ha.

NORMAN. She brought the laundry, too.

TONY. Good. I could use a shirt. It's pretty bad walking around all day without being able to take off your coat. *(Takes off coat—has no shirt under it. Picks out blue shirt from laundry that* NORMAN *is sorting.)*

GEORGE. *(Iron mask business. Through his hands)* Ah-ah.

TONY. *(Throws it down—takes another)* It's too big around the neck anyway. *(Sees* GEORGE'S *agonised expression)* What's the matter with you?

GEORGE. I'm the Man in the Iron Mask.

TONY. Oh—Stanislavsky, Chapter Two. Anything doing today, Norman? *(Goes up; looks on bulletin board.)*

NORMAN. I had a long talk with Brock Pemberton about the juvenile in his new show.

TONY. *(Crossing down* R.) What did he say? *(*NORMAN *juts out his chin; scowls and shakes his head)* Yeah—that's what he just said to me. *(Exits to bedroom* R. *with shirt; closes door after him.)*

NORMAN. Say, George, did you have two pairs of shorts in the laundry this week?

GEORGE. *(Pulling out his pants to see)* Who, me? No—one.

NORMAN. Must be Tony, then. *(Motions* GEORGE *over)* Say, George—what about Tony?

GEORGE. What about him?

(The DOORBELL rings. GEORGE *goes to press the buzzer.)*

NORMAN. Haven't you noticed anything? Wouldn't you say that Tony and Marge were—well, haven't you noticed anything?

GEORGE. What sort of thing?

NORMAN. They act like they're in love. We can't have anything like that going on around here.

GEORGE. No, that would be bad.

NORMAN. People might talk. We'll have to make them snap out of it. *(Starts off* L.I *with laundry.)*

GEORGE. Say, Norman—I can't do the Iron Mask.

NORMAN. Well, take anything—the sofa—and pretend it's something else—your boat. That's it! You're in a rowboat—miles from shore—and slowly dying of thirst.

GEORGE. Yeah.

NORMAN. *(As he exits—pleased with himself) Miles* from shore.

GEORGE. *(Climbs onto the sofa, settles himself and starts acting the problem* NORMAN *described. There is a KNOCK at the door)* Come in.

MURIEL. (MURIEL FOSTER *sticks her head in* C. *She is a rather prim girl, naive but suspicious)* Oh— excuse me. *(She partially closes the door, then opens it again, fascinated by what* GEORGE *is doing)* This must be the wrong apartment. I'm looking for Dottie Coburn.

GEORGE. *(Exhausted)* This is it. (MURIEL *comes in)* You want to row a while? I'm tired.

MURIEL. Row?

GEORGE. This is a rowboat.

MURIEL. No, I just want to see Dottie— (TONY *enters from bedroom* R.*—gets manuscript from bookcase, takes chair down* R., *sits, studies)* Is Dottie Coburn here?

NORMAN. *(Enters)* Did you pay for the laundry?

GEORGE. No.

NORMAN. *(Crossing to* C.*)* There's an extra girdle in it this week. *(Holds up girdle)* Is it yours? *(He looks up; discovers* MURIEL *isn't one of the three girls.)*

MURIEL. Gracious, no!

NORMAN. I guess it's a mistake, then.

GEORGE. Maybe you put an extra one in.

NORMAN. *(Crossing* R.*)* No, I didn't. I counted every piece. I don't know why I always have to tend

to the laundry. *(Starts to go, then indicates* MURIEL*)*
Who's that?

GEORGE. Probably a spy. (NORMAN *exits* L.1, *satisfied.* GEORGE *turns to* MURIEL*)* Who sent you? .

MURIEL. Why—why, no one sent me. I dropped in to see Dottie. Are you sure this is her apartment?

GEORGE. Let me see— *(Crossing up* L.C.—*puts sweater on rack)* She pays the rent—occasionally. The phone is in her name, and the lease, so I guess it's hers all right. We're all just visiting.

MURIEL. What do you mean, we all? Who else lives here?

GEORGE. Well, I do—and Norman—that's Norman in there with the girdle— (MURIEL *jumps guiltily)* and Dotty and Tony and Marge and Kate.

MURIEL. You all live here? In one apartment?

GEORGE. Now you're getting it. *(Goes to trunk down* L.*)*

MURIEL. But what will people say?

GEORGE. I can't imagine. *(Sits on trunk.* NORMAN *enters; thumb-tacks laundry list onto bulletin board)* Norman! Hey, Norman!

NORMAN. Hm?

GEORGE. What will people say?

NORMAN. *(Evidently this has been asked before)* My dear young lady, what possible harm can result from the fact that three boys and three girls share the same apartment? We have banded together for financial reasons—period! *(Exits* R.*)*

GEORGE. Thank you. He's the official explainer.

MURIEL. Oh, but I wasn't thinking anything like—

(KATE *and* MARGE *are heard off up* C.)

GEORGE. *(Sitting up)* No—no.

MURIEL. *(Retreats* R.*)* Oh, but really— *(As the* GIRLS *enter she backs downstage and sits on sofa.)*

(The door c. opens, and MURIEL *is interrupted by the entrance of* KATE *and* MARGE. MARGE *is young and attractive—a little more serious than the others.* KATE *is the cynic of the crowd, tall and dark.)*

KATE. *(Off)* I don't know what good it will do us, but there he is.

MARGE. *(Off)* Of course it's important. He may be here longer this time.

KATE. (KATE *enters, followed by* MARGE*)* So what he'll do is brush us off again.

MARGE. *(Closes door—on step)* But we can't let him. He must be human. He has to listen. Tony, it's Mr. Kenny.

TONY. *(Rises; goes up)* Are you sure it's Mr. Kenny?

(The GIRLS *hang up their coats.* KATE *puts bag, gloves on bench.)*

KATE. No one but a producer could look that much like an undertaker.

GEORGE. Mr. Kenny?

MARGE. Yes, George—he's back. He's downstairs. His door was open and we saw him.

KATE. That's about as close as we'll ever get to him.

MARGE. Oh, I know he'll see us, I know he will—he has to.

TONY. But, Marge—we tried to see him six *weeks* ago—before he *went* to Florida—

MARGE. We just have to *keep* trying.

GEORGE. Well—why doesn't somebody take a look, then?

TONY. *(Puts book on pillow; crosses down* R. *to radiator; looks through hole in floor where pipe comes up)* You mean me, I suppose. I hope Mrs.

Garnet never finds out about these pipes.—Hey—the lights *are* on down here.

KATE. It was Kenny, all right. *(Goes to bookcase; opens letter she finds on bulletin board.)*

(Enter NORMAN with kitchen towels from laundry; drops them on table.)

GEORGE. Norman—Kenny's back. *(To MARGE)* He couldn't stay in Florida forever.

NORMAN. *(Crossing L.)* Really?

GEORGE. Sure! Tony says there's a light downstairs.

NORMAN. *(He lies on the floor by the radiator L and pulls the pipe away)* There's a light here, too *(More excited)* There's somebody down there.

MARGE. What's he doing? *(Goes L.)*

KATE. What's down there, anyway?

NORMAN. Looks like a bedroom. I can see part of a bed.

GEORGE. Sounds reasonable.

(MURIEL rises.)

NORMAN. And a foot—he's putting on slippers—red slippers. What do you know about that?

MARGE. Is it Mr. Kenny?

NORMAN. I don't know. This is strictly a bird's eye view. He has a head. It's moving. Now it's gone. Why doesn't he stay put?

GEORGE. If we had a saw—

KATE. No, George—we could *not* saw through the floor.

TONY. *(Still at radiator down R.)* I can see him now—almost.

(ALL cross R. NORMAN walks over sofa. GEORGE pushes MURIEL down onto sofa.)

GEORGE. Don't get up. We're very informal here.

MURIEL. But what are they all looking at?

GEORGE. The future—we hope. *(Goes to radiator and pushes* TONY *aside)* Here, let me look. *(Peers through hole)* Gosh—I could spit right on him.

KATE. Well—don't.

GEORGE. But I've never spit on a producer before.

MARGE. In his office they said he wouldn't be back for weeks, and they weren't doing any casting for months.

KATE. You're lucky that blonde witch didn't tell you to come back in 1945.

NORMAN. Don't be bitter, pet.

KATE. Why not? I think it's a crime when you have to pull stunts like this to see a producer. *(Goes* L. *Gets slippers from off* L.I.*)*

GEORGE. And at that—through a peephole.

TONY. Listen, George—producers wouldn't have time to do any shows if they saw all the people who wanted to be in them.

*(*KATE *crosses down* L.*)*

MARGE. Tony's right. After all, in the theater—

MURIEL. *(Jumping to her feet eagerly)* Oh—are you all actors?

(They ALL *turn and stare at her strangely.)*

KATE. *(Stops)* Who is that?

NORMAN. I don't know. She's a friend of George's.

GEORGE. No, she isn't. I never saw her before in my life.

TONY. How'd she get in here?

MARGE. How long has she been here?

*(*KATE *sits on trunk; changes into slippers.)*

GEORGE. Maybe she's always been here, and we've never noticed her.

(NORMAN *taps her shoulder; she turns* L. GEORGE *taps her* R. *shoulder; she turns* R., *frightened.*)

NORMAN. I beg your pardon—are you in show business?
MURIEL. Why, no—
NORMAN. Wait—don't speak.

(They ALL *crowd around* MURIEL, *examining her curiously.)*

GEORGE. Have you ever tried radio?
TONY. Or pictures?
MARGE. Or television?
NORMAN. Or castor-oil?
MURIEL. No, you don't understand. I—
TONY. What have I seen you in?
MARGE. What experience have you had?
NORMAN. What do you have to *give* the theater?
GEORGE. Why do *you* want to be an actress?
MURIEL. I don't—
GEORGE. She says she doesn't.
NORMAN. It's an act. She's playing hard to get.
TONY. Do you think she's exactly the type?
GEORGE. Mm—she might do.
MARGE. *(To* MURIEL*)* Do you speak French?
MURIEL. Yes, I do.
GEORGE. Too bad—we were looking for someone who *couldn't* speak French.
NORMAN. You'll have to come back later.

(KATE *rises—crosses in.*)

TONY. *(Going up* L.*)* Be sure and leave your name and telephone number, so we'll know where *not* to call.
MARGE. *(Walking her to door)* Come and see us sometime—anytime.

MURIEL. *(Jerking away and facing them)* I think you're all horrid.

KATE. *(Breaking it up. Pushes NORMAN to down R.)* All right, kids. That's your exit cue. Now beat it and leave the girl alone.

(TONY and MARGE exit L.2 to kitchen.)

GEORGE. *(Crossing down R. to sofa, sits)* That's gratitude for you. After we tried to help her, too.

KATE. You might start getting supper ready.

(NORMAN goes to below bookcase.)

GEORGE. *(Lying down on sofa)* We can't. There aren't any clean dishes.

NORMAN. Come on, I'll help you. Nothing would ever get done around here if I didn't tend to it.

(They exit L.2.)

KATE. *(Opening door)* You mustn't mind them.

MURIEL. I think they're all crazy.

KATE. No—they're actors.

MURIEL. Just because you're actors, you don't have to be that crazy.

KATE. It helps.

MURIEL. I don't know what Dottie's father would think—

KATE. Dottie's father? *(Closes door)* Oh—you're a friend of Dottie's! *(Overly cordial)* Well—come right in. We're always delighted to see any friend of hers. *(Fixes chair L.C. for her)* Can I take your things?

MURIEL. *(Sits)* No, thank you.

KATE. You know—I still don't know your name. I'm Kate Ault.

MURIEL. I'm Muriel Foster. I went to school with

Dottie in Boston—at Miss Wheelock's. I saw Dottie's father yesterday, and he didn't know anything about this.

KATE. About what?

MURIEL. Well—those three boys; they certainly are rude.

KATE. No, they're not. They're just scared. *(Sits on trunk)* So am I. We try to cover it up.

MURIEL. What is there to be scared of?

KATE. Oh—that we're not as good as we think we are—that somewhere, sometime, somebody might do a play that has the part for us in it, and we won't be there to get it.

MURIEL. But there are so many parts—

KATE. There are a lot of us, too. Maybe some of us shouldn't be here. I think that's what we're most scared of—that we'll find out we just don't belong.

MURIEL. But why do you live here like this?

KATE. Well, we found out Arthur Kenny, the producer, lived downstairs, and we wanted to meet him—

MURIEL. Why does a big producer like Mr. Kenny want to live in a cheap place like this?

KATE. He thinks it's lucky. He lived here when he produced his hit.

MURIEL. Well, all I can say is, it's a funny way to get jobs.

KATE. *(Rises, crossing in)* Walter Huston said, "If you can't get into the theater by beating on closed doors with your fists, use your head."

MURIEL. Why is it any better to beat on a door with your head?

KATE. I wouldn't worry about it if I were you. Our heads are pretty hard.

(On cue "heads" the c. door opens and DOTTIE COBURN enters. She is a petite blonde girl, young and attractive—always a little vague.

*She has a package with her, and she is breath-
less with pent up excitement. She drops beret
and package onto bookcase. Peers off R. while
removing coat, which she drops onto head of
sofa.)*

DOTTIE. Kate! Guess what!

KATE. You've got a job.

DOTTIE. Oh, no—it isn't that. *(Removes trench
coat; drops it on head sofa.)*

MURIEL. *(Getting up)* Hello, Dottie—

DOTTIE. *(Not realizing who it is)* Hello! *(To
KATE)* It's the most wonderful thing! Where *is*
everyone? I want to tell them all.

KATE. They're out in the kitchen. *(Calling)* Hey,
kids, Dottie's got some news.

DOTTTIE. *(Picks up package and crosses to
kitchen. Pushing on door)* I can't tell you how
thrilled I was.

MURIEL. Dottie, you might at least
say—

NORMAN. *(Coming in with OTHERS,
wearing red apron. As he enters DOT-
TIE retreats R.)* Did you bring the hamburgers?

(Together)

*(MARGE follows him on; moves downstage toward
chair; then GEORGE, who goes to C.)*

DOTTIE. No, it isn't that.

KATE. Don't tell me you brought steak.

GEORGE. What'd you bring?

(MURIEL turns away down L., peeved.)

DOTTIE. Be quiet, all of you. You won't even care
about food when I tell you what I know.

TONY. *(Entering)* What's the matter?

DOTTIE. *(With dramatic emphasis)* I know this is absolutely true—Arthur Kenny is back! He's downstairs right now! Isn't that wonderful? (MARGE *sits.* TONY *goes* L. *to radiator. They make faces of disgust)* Well—isn't it?

NORMAN. Good old Dottie! Back in the flesh—with the *flesh. (Goes off to kitchen* L.2.)

(GEORGE *goes* R.—*lies on sofa.)*

DOTTIE. *(Crossing to* MARGE. *Weakly, but still determined)* It's Arthur Kenny—the producer—he's here.

MARGE. We've been spying on him through the radiator holes, Dottie.

DOTTIE. Oh—oh, then you knew it. It wasn't a surprise.

MURIEL. *(Crossing up* C.) Dottie Coburn, if you haven't any more manners than these—these friends of yours—

DOTTIE. *(Embracing her)* Why, Muriel—darling! When did you get in town? Do you know all these people?

MURIEL. Well enough, thank you.

DOTTIE. You'll stay for dinner, won't you?

GEORGE. Wait a minute—how many hamburgers did you bring?

DOTTIE. Six—I always bring six. *(Explaining to* MURIEL) There are six of us here, you know, so we need six hamburgers. That's one for each person—isn't it?

MURIEL. Then obviously I can't stay.

GEORGE. Intelligent girl.

KATE. Almost.

MARGE. Of course you can stay. One of us can get a bite to eat around the corner.

TONY. Dottie, if a friend of mine suddenly appeared in town, I'd take her *out* some place to dinner.

DOTTIE. Oh, that's a lovely idea. Why don't you take her around to Schrafft's? *(Pushes* MURIEL *toward him.)*

TONY. Dottie, I said a friend of *mine*. *(Sits on radiator.)*

KATE. *(Helping* DOTTIE *into her coat)* Look—if you two are going, you'd better go now. Because don't forget, we're going to rehearse tonight, Dottie.

DOTTIE. You could start with the second act. *(To* MURIEL*)* That's when I'm unconscious.

TONY. I think we ought to run through. We've got to be ready if Mr. Kenny wants to see it.

GEORGE. What makes you think Mr. Kenny *will* want to see it?

MARGE. *(Rises)* He's got to see it, that's all.

DOTTIE. Why don't I stop by and ask him tonight?

KATE. No, Dottie— Not tonight, and not you— ever.

DOTTIE. Well—I'll try to think of something. That won't hurt, will it? *(Starts up.)*

KATE. *(Crossing to sofa)* I don't know, Dottie—it might.

(DOTTIE *goes up* C.)

MARGE. Goodbye, Muriel! See that Dottie comes back soon.

MURIEL. I'm not sure she ought to come back at all. If Mr. Coburn knew about this—

KATE. But he doesn't know.

MURIEL. I said *if* he knew— *(Her voice trails off weakly as* KATE *approaches)* he'd be terribly upset.

KATE. *(With meaning)* But he's not going to know—is he, dear?

MURIEL. Well—it's none of my business if Dottie wants to live like a—a—

GEORGE. A communist?
MURIEL. I wouldn't know about that.

(KATE *goes up* C.)

TONY. No—*you* wouldn't.
GEORGE. But someday you might— *(Approaching her with a definite leer; unbuttoning his shirt.* KATE *opens the* C. *door)* Why not now?
MURIEL. Oh-oh—I have to go. Come on, Dottie. *(She exits hurriedly—pulling* DOTTIE *after her.)*
DOTTIE. *(Laughing)* Oh, George!

(KATE *closes door.*)

MARGE. That girl could make plenty of trouble if she wanted to.
KATE. And I think she wants to.
GEORGE. There's no use worrying about it. I'm going out and divide up that extra hamburger. *(He exits* L.2.*)*
KATE. Oh, no, not by yourself you're not. *(Exits* L.2.*)*

(MARGE *starts to follow them out.* TONY *stops her; pulls her to him; speaks quietly.)*

TONY. Hello!
MARGE. Hello, Tony!

(They kiss tenderly, then TONY *glances briefly off* L. *and joins* MARGE *at radiator* L.*)*

TONY. You know, Marge, it would be easier pretending to be married than it is being married and pretending not to be. I hate this business of sneaking kisses behind people's backs.
MARGE. *(Reproachfully)* Tony.

TONY. I'm sorry. You don't like it, do you?

MARGE. You know I don't.

TONY. It makes it seem so cheap.

MARGE. Nothing could make our marriage seem cheap, Tony. It's wonderful and beautiful.

TONY. That's the way I want to make it for you, darling. But why can't we tell the kids?

MARGE. You might as well have it flashed on the news ticker at Times Square. And then Aunt Mabel would worry so—because we don't have jobs, and I just couldn't take another thing from her. She's been so sweet to me already.

TONY. I guess you're right. We haven't had any money for weeks.

MARGE. Dottie's the only one who has any, and I hate to keep sponging on her.

TONY. How do you think I feel?

MARGE. I know, darling. Tony, you're not sorry, are you?

TONY. About us? No, Marge, never.

MARGE. If only our play hadn't closed—

TONY. You'd think you could afford to get married after eighteen curtain calls. People cheered and whistled. I didn't know a person could have as many relatives as that Hollywood star had in the audience.

MARGE. I guess we should have waited to read the reviews.

TONY. *(Crossing to* MARGE*)* I'm glad we didn't.

MARGE. So am I, darling. I love being your wife, even if we do have to keep it a secret. But it won't be long, Tony. You'll get a job soon—I know you will. You'll get a wonderful job, and we'll go to Hollywood and be rich.

TONY. I wish I were as sure as you are.

MARGE. You have to be, Tony. You have to be confident and have faith in yourself. After all, the theater's your business. You've got notices.

TONY. Yeah, but you can't eat notices—not even Winchell on toast.

MARGE. Darling, that reminds me. We ought to be setting the table.

(The rest moves rapidly. MARGE gets three cushions from the trunk and carries them R. TONY straightens the sofa, then pulls down the bookcase and places it flat on the floor. A fancy frilled white cloth is painted on the back of the bookcase.)

TONY. All right, you get the chairs—I'll get the table.

MARGE. Coming up—chairs for the gentlemen.

TONY. Coming down—one table. You know—this tablecloth is getting dirty. We ought to paint another one on.

KATE. *(Enters L.2 with five plates; gets silverware from table)* Haven't you done that yet?

GEORGE. *(Enters with catsup bottle; wears apron)* I'm so hungry I could eat a horse. *(Sits on chair L.C.)*

KATE. Don't say things like that! *(Knocks on table.)*

(NORMAN enters L.2 with platter of hamburgers and watches TONY.)

TONY. *(Helping MARGE onto cushion)* I *think* I forgot to eat lunch today.

MARGE. Tony! You shouldn't.

NORMAN. *(To GEORGE)* There, see what I mean? An opportunity like that, and he didn't pinch her. He's in love.

(ALL except GEORGE sit at table.)

GEORGE. *(Crossing R.)* I'll bet Mr. Kenny's downstairs right now eating roast squab.

NORMAN. You'll eat hamburger and like it.

KATE. I always say the theater is so glamorous.

(WARN Curtain.)

NORMAN. I have a brief announcement to make. You know the radio commercial I was going to do? Well, I didn't get the job.

(GEORGE sits head sofa.)

MARGE. Oh, Norman—

NORMAN. It seems my voice was too light—and too heavy—and too smooth and too rough.

KATE. I wasn't the type in sixteen offices today.

GEORGE. Yeah—me, too.

TONY. I'm getting pretty well fed up with the glamorous theater. I'm going to get out of it and find myself a job—any kind of a job so I can make some money.

MARGE. Tony, you're going to be a fine actor. You mustn't talk like that.

KATE. Why not? It's what we'd all do if we had any sense.

MARGE. I think you're being childish. Doesn't it mean anything to you that Mr. Kenny's back?

KATE. Yeah—it means I'll get thrown out of his office tomorrow.

TONY. Kenny doesn't even know we're alive.

NORMAN. Now cut it out—all of you. You're just discouraged. I'm discouraged too, but that doesn't matter. We can't get out of the theater. We *are* the theater. We're actors and we're going to be good ones, too.

KATE. If anybody will give us a chance.

GEORGE. At least we can eat *now*.

KATE. Norman, will you say grace?

(ALL *bow their heads reverently.*)

NORMAN. Dear God, please send us a producer.

CURTAIN

ACT ONE

SCENE II

The scene is the same, except that the table is once more a bookcase. It is Saturday morning after breakfast.

The bedroom doors are open. There is a cup and saucer on R. radiator and one on table. Sunlight streams through Left bedroom doorway.
TONY, *in bathroom, is vocalizing.*

At rise, GEORGE *enters from Right in hat and overcoat, pounds on the bathroom door, shouting to be heard, and starts looking for phone book. Finds it under Left end of sofa.*

DOTTIE *is discovered picking cushion off floor —puts it on sofa and begins dusting sofa. She wears slacks. She pulls cup, saucer out from under Right end sofa.*

GEORGE. I still think it was a dirty trick, Tony. It was my turn to take a bath this morning.

TONY. *(From bathroom)* What?

GEORGE. I said it was a dirty trick—dirty—dirty —dirty!

TONY. Why don't you take a bath?

GEORGE. *(Sits on step looking for address in phone book)* How? You knew I needed a bath. I have an appointment.

TONY. I'll be through in an hour or so. *(Resumes his vocalizing.)*

GEORGE. It's a fine thing when you can't even bathe in your own bathtub.

DOTTIE. George, Muriel said you were very, very rude to her.

GEORGE. Not nearly enough.

DOTTIE. She said she had a surprise for us, but she wouldn't tell me what it was.

GEORGE. Maybe she has leprosy.

NORMAN. *(Entering from R. bedroom, carries pad, pencil on ear; gets cups, saucers from below sofa end of radiator, R.; puts them on table)* Where do you think you're going? It's your turn to make the beds this morning.

GEORGE. I got breakfast—Tony makes the beds— if he ever finishes bathing—

DOTTIE. Let's see what's on the bulletin board. *(Crossing up to bulletin board.)*

GEORGE. What for?

NORMAN. That's funny—it looks like something's been erased.

GEORGE. No, it doesn't.

NORMAN. Yes—now, how could that have happened?

(DOTTIE *sits sofa.*)

GEORGE. Sabotage.

NORMAN. All right. For that you wash the dishes every night this week.

GEORGE. I was just trying to write my name down for extra work. Can I help it if I used the wrong end of the pencil? *(Tears page from book. Drops book; exits.)*

(TONY's *singing fades away.*)

NORMAN. *(Puts book into bookcase. Closing door*

R.) You must think we're awful heels, Dottie—letting you pay for all our food.

DOTTIE. You chip in everything you make.

NORMAN. That hasn't been much lately.

DOTTIE. I don't care. I want to be with you—I mean, with all of you. That's why I'm always afraid Daddy might find out I lend you his money. I don't think he'd like it.

NORMAN. *(Goes to bookcase and works)* I guess it's a little different from life in Boston.

DOTTIE. *(Sitting sofa; facing front)* Norman, do you think I'm ignorant?

NORMAN. No, Dottie—just dumb.

DOTTIE. Oh, well, that's all right. Muriel said I was ignorant.

NORMAN. For. my money, Muriel talks too much.

DOTTIE. She said I was too ignorant to be a good actress.

NORMAN. *(Coming down to foot of sofa)* It always amazes me how good you are, Dottie. I can't understand it myself, but the minute you get on a stage, you're a different person. It just goes to show, you don't need brains to act.

DOTTIE. Of course not. Look at Pinochio.

NORMAN. Yeah, that's what I meant.

DOTTIE. Norman, I think I'd die if I couldn't be in New York. At least I feel closer to the theater here than I would in Boston.

NORMAN. I guess we're a pretty screwy bunch, but anyway we know what we're after—and we're all after it pretty desperately.

DOTTIE. That's what I tried to tell Muriel, but she couldn't understand.

NORMAN. No one not in the theater can understand why it means so much to the ones in it.

DOTTIE. I want it more than anything else in the world. Even if I never get any closer to it than this, I still want it.

NORMAN. So do I. All we need is a break.

DOTTIE. I hope you get one, Norman. You deserve it more than any of us. You don't even think about anything else, do you?

NORMAN. What else is there?

DOTTIE. Oh—nothing, I guess. (NORMAN *goes up to bulletin board*) It's just that—well, never mind.

NORMAN. What are you mumbling about?

DOTTIE. It wasn't important. *(A pause)* I wish—

NORMAN. What?

DOTTIE. *(Crossing to* R. *end of bookcase)* I wish we could get jobs in the same show, Norman, and that it would run forever—like Tobacco Road did.

NORMAN. Not me—turnips give me indigestion. Anyway, that kept running only because it got banned in Chicago.

DOTTIE. Maybe someday we could get banned.

NORMAN. Fat chance. *(Goes up* R.—*gets dishes off table.* TONY *begins vocalizing)* Come on—I'll help you with the breakfast dishes.

DOTTIE. *(Crossing up* R.) Why couldn't we use paper dishes? Then they wouldn't be so much trouble to wash.

NORMAN. *(As they exit* L.2) Sure—just wring them out and hang them up to dry.

(TONY, *wearing tie and sweater, comes out of bath-room* R. *and goes down* R. *to radiator. He spies through hole. After a moment* MARGE *comes from room* L.I.)

MARGE. *(Going to* TONY) Is he down there?

TONY. No, but I got a glimpse of him earlier. He had an apron on.

MARGE. He must be cooking something—something exotic.

TONY. Maybe he's a Mason.

MARGE. No—he's quite an authority on foods—a

member of the Escoffiers or Gourmets or something. Didn't you know that?

TONY. I'm dumb. The only thing I know is that I love you.

MARGE. Don't ever stop loving me, Tony.

TONY. Don't worry.

MARGE. If only Mr. Kenny will see our show, and if only he likes us—

(The TELEPHONE rings.)

TONY. *(Going to answer)* We've got to get him up here. That's all there is to it. *(Into phone)* Hello— Yes— I said yes, do you want to speak to her? —Just a minute— What's that?—Yes, this is Miss Coburn's apartment— You what?—Oh, you're Mr. Coburn—Dottie's father?—Me?—I'm Anthony—uh —Anthony. *(Gradually he develops a thick Irish accent)* Sure, and it's the janitor I am. It's after fixing the leak in the radiator I've come up about. Sure, sure—and I'm thinking you'd be after speaking to the little chicadee, Miss Coburn, Begorrah, Erin go bragh, (MARGE *tries to stop him*) shamrocks and shillelahs! I'll fetch her! *(Putting hand over mouthpiece and calling out)* Dottie—phone. *(To MARGE)* It's her father.

MARGE. *(Starts L.)* Did he think it was funny your answering?

TONY. Hilarious! Do you know any more Irish?

MARGE. *(Crossing L.)* For Heaven's sake, don't do any more.

DOTTIE. *(Coming in L.2; carrying a dish towel)* What did you say?

TONY. Telephone—it's your father.

DOTTIE. Silly, it can't be. He's in Boston. He wouldn't call until after seven o'clock.

(MARGE moves her R.; sits her end sofa.)

TONY. Dottie, it's your father, and he's not in Boston. It sounded like he was right around the corner.

MARGE. Look, Dottie—be very careful. He mightn't understand about all of us being here.

DOTTIE. *(Into phone)* Hello— Why, Daddy— Where are you?—At the station?

MARGE. *(Crossing to bedroom door L.1)* Kate! Kate! *(Exits for a second; returns; exits L.2. Pause. Returns.)*

DOTTIE. Yes, that was Tony who answered the telephone— Tony? Oh, he's—

TONY. *(Whispering)* I'm the janitor.

DOTTIE. He *says* he's the janitor. Why, of course not, Daddy—

MARGE. *(She has called* KATE *and* NORMAN *into the room)* Kids—keep your fingers crossed. It's Dottie's father.

NORMAN. In New York?

MARGE. Yes.

KATE. What'll we do?

DOTTIE. No, Daddy, that's silly— Well, you can come right over and see for yourself.

NORMAN. *(Takes phone; is about to speak; returns it)* Goodbye. Come on, Tony. *(Starts for C. door, dragging* TONY *with him.)*

MARGE. Wait a minute—what about your clothes?

DOTTIE. But, Daddy—a taxi could get you over here in five minutes.

NORMAN. *(To* DOTTIE*)* Tell him to walk—it's good exercise.

DOTTIE. You ought to walk, Daddy—it's good exercise. All right, Daddy, fine. Hurry up as— *(*NORMAN *pokes her)* as slow as you can. *(*TONY *puts phone on bookcase. Rises)* Isn't it wonderful? *(Crossing to* KATE*)* Daddy's coming right over.

KATE. *(Crossing L.C.)* That's just lovely.

MARGE. *(Coming down)* We can't stand around

like this. We've got to do something. If we lose Dottie, we won't eat.

TONY. *(Runs L.)* Come on, Norman. Let's pack our clothes and get out of here. *(Pulls trunk to C.)*

(KATE *throws pillows off trunk.*)

NORMAN. It won't take long to pack mine.

MARGE. And your shaving things—don't forget them.

KATE. You could tell him I'm a bearded lady. *(Goes up L.C. for overcoat and scarf—puts them into trunk.)*

(MARGE *exits bathroom.*)

DOTTIE. *(Crossing L. to* KATE*)* I wonder what Daddy's doing in New York?

NORMAN. You don't suppose he heard anything, do you?

MARGE. How could he? *(Drops shaving things into trunk.)*

KATE. What about Muriel?

MARGE. She said she knew him. *(Throws towel from her shoulder into trunk.)*

NORMAN. The little stinker!

DOTTIE. I'm sure he doesn't know. He would have sounded mad instead of just apoplectic.

TONY. Norman—what are you waiting for? Bring me some clothes.

(KATE *crosses to* L. *of* DOTTIE.)

NORMAN. *(Exiting to bedroom* R.*)* You mean everything—both shirts?

(The following packing business must go as rapidly as possible—frantically—madly.)

MARGE. *(Crossing to rack)* Look—what about this fencing stuff? He might pry around.

KATE. Do you think Dottie ought to have on slacks? It looks sort of masculine.

MARGE. Dottie, go put on a dress—very frilly. *(DOTTIE and KATE exit L.1)* We'll make him think she's better taken care of here than she could be anywhere else.

NORMAN. *(Puts coat on off stage. Running out with big bundle of clothes—dumps them into trunk)* Here—and don't be too particular packing them— except my tuxedo.

TONY. What about George's things?

NORMAN. Lord, yes! *(Exits R.)*

MARGE. Are you sure this is everything?

TONY. I'm surprised we had this much. It's only because the laundry came back yesterday.

NORMAN. *(Coming in with one blue shirt and one sock; wears hat and coat)* Here are George's things.

MARGE. Well, put them in. What about his pa-jamas?

TONY. It's cold out. He's probably still got them on.

(MARGE *goes up* R. *to table.*)

NORMAN. Bathrobe—I just remembered. *(Exits R.)*

MARGE. Here are some pipes. Put them in, too. *(Throws them to TONY)* Oh! And the overshoes in the kitchen. *(Runs out L.2.)*

NORMAN. *(Returns, bringing in bathrobe and pair of pajamas)* Here—throw these in.

TONY. Where's George's bathrobe?

NORMAN. Oh, yes— *(Calling off L.2 door)* Marge, bring in George's bathrobe. It's in the breadbox.

TONY. What's it doing there?

NORMAN. It keeps the bread fresh.

DOTTIE. *(Coming in* L.1 *with dress.* KATE *enters with her)* Do you think this dress is all right?

TONY. Lovely, but can't you fix your hair?

(DOTTIE *runs off* L.1.)

MARGE. *(Bringing in overshoes and bathrobe from* L.2*)* Here's some more stuff.

KATE. Pipes! *(Crosses up* R. *to table.)*

TONY. If Dottie's father finds out anything, he's liable to get sore.

NORMAN. And without Dottie, we'd be sunk.

(KATE *takes down bulletin board.)*

TONY. *(Stands in trunk and tramples clothes down flat)* What about the rent? Don't let him know about that.

MARGE. I'm sure it will be all right.

NORMAN. I'd feel a lot better if we could gag Dottie.

KATE. *(Putting bulletin board under sofa)* I'll watch every move she makes.

TONY. Tell her father that you chaperone her every minute.

DOTTIE. *(Coming in with pants)* What'll I do with these?

TONY. Here. *(Throws them into trunk.)*

DOTTIE. But they're mine.

NORMAN. It doesn't matter—they're pants.

TONY. Is this everything?

MARGE. *(Going off* R.*)* I'll make sure.

KATE. *(Running into bathroom. Returning with towels)* These towels—put them in.

DOTTIE. Can't girls use towels?

KATE. Not when they're marked Y.M.C.A. *(She crosses* R.*)*

DOTTIE. Oh!

MARGE. *(Coming from* R. *with* TONY'S *coat and hat)* It looks all right. I didn't see anything. You better hurry. He'll be here any minute. *(Closes bathroom door, then closes door* R.*)*

NORMAN. *(Helping* TONY *close trunk)* We'll go across the street to the drugstore. Then we can see when he leaves.

TONY. Whatever you do—don't let him take Dottie away with him.

NORMAN. Tell him anything. *(With* TONY, *he picks up the trunk)* We can leave this under the stairs outside.

(As they approach the C. *door a loud KNOCK is heard. They stare at one another aghast.)*

MARGE. How did he get here so fast?

KATE. It couldn't be—

NORMAN. Just the same, it might be. *(Drops the trunk.)*

(Suddenly the two BOYS *go into action—but quietly.* TONY *rushes over to the radiator* L. *and takes off his shoe.* NORMAN *follows suit.)*

MARGE. *(Indicating door)* Dottie—

KATE. No—she shouldn't be doing anything. *(Hustles* DOTTIE *to sofa)* Marge—go ahead. *(To* DOTTIE*)* Now, Dottie, we want your father to know you're happy. So try to *look happy.*

*(*DOTTIE *grins vacantly.* TONY *starts pounding on the radiator with his shoe, singing very loudly, "When Irish Eyes Are Smiling."* NORMAN *follows suit. After a moment* MARGE *goes gingerly to the door and opens it.* MRS. GARNET, *the landlady, comes in and looks at them calmly; direcs and sings with them.* TONY *finally sees*

who it is and stops in disgust. So does NOR-
MAN.)

MRS. GARNET. That's very pretty. I love music.
TONY. For the love of God!
NORMAN. Why don't you knock when it's you?
MRS. GARNET. I did knock.
NORMAN. Then don't.
MARGE. What is it, Mrs. Garnet?
MRS. GARNET. *(Apologetically)* It's about the
rent.
MARGE. Oh—the rent.
MRS. GARNET. Yes. *(Goes to* DOTTIE*)* Miss Co-
burn— (DOTTIE *is still grinning vacantly)* Miss
Co— *(To* OTHERS*)* Is anything the matter with her?
DOTTIE. I'm happy.
MRS. GARNET. She looks queer.
NORMAN. *(Crossing* R. *to* MRS. GARNET*)* Yes—
she—she's had a terrible shock.
KATE. So have I.
NORMAN. But I mean about the accident—and her
father.
DOTTIE. What accident?
NORMAN. *(Crossing to* DOTTIE*)* The accident he
was in when he was rushing to the bedside of his
dying brother—Stanislavsky.
KATE. Yes, Mr. Coburn's brother in Oklahoma.
NORMAN. And the car got smashed up and you
had to send him the money to get out of jail—our
rent money—and that's why we're a little slow about
paying it—remember?
DOTTIE. No.
KATE. You see—she's still delirious. Believe me,
Mrs. Garnet, it was awful.
MARGE. We had visions of blood all over the place.
TONY. From the shattered windshield, you know?
MRS. GARNET. Heavens, how horrible! Of course
she's upset.

KATE. Naturally, we had to send him the money right away.

MRS. GARNET. Why, yes. You did perfectly right.

DOTTIE. *(To* KATE*)* What happened to the money I gave you last week—

(NORMAN *puts his hat over her face.)*

MARGE. You see, Mrs. Garnet, she can't even think straight.

MRS. GARNET. The poor child. I know just what she needs. *(Crossing up)* Salts! *(Exits* C.*)*

NORMAN. Where are we going to find the rent money?

TONY. Never mind that now. Come on—let's get out of here!

(The DOORBELL rings. Immediately the two
      BOYS *starts to go back into their acts.* MARGE
      stops them.)

MARGE. No—you can still make it. Go up to the next floor, and wait until he comes in here.

NORMAN. O.K.! Then we'll go over to the drugstore. *(With* TONY *he picks up the trunks, and they exit* C.*)*

(The DOORBELL rings again imperatively. KATE
      closes door.)

MARGE. Can't somebody say a prayer or something?

KATE. *(Presses buzzer)* What do you think I'm doing?

DOTTIE. Do you want me to look happy again?

MARGE. Dottie, please make him let you stay here Tell him how much you love it—how you'd be miserable anywhere else.

KATE. You needn't mention how we have to eat.

DOTTIE. But I do love it here. I don't want to go anywhere else.

MARGE. That's it—only put more pathos in it.

DOTTIE. *(Acting)* I love it here.

MARGE. That's better.

(There is a KNOCK at the door.)

KATE. *(Going to answer)* Dottie—remember to think before you speak— *(Crossing up)* —and, if possible—don't speak. *(She opens the door and admits* MR. COBURN. *He is a successful business man turned politician, a Rotarian and healthy.)*

COBURN. How do you do? Does Miss Coburn live here?

KATE. Yes. Won't you come in?

DOTTIE. *(Jumping up to greet him)* Oh, Daddy!

COBURN. Hello, darling!

DOTTIE. I'm so glad to see you.

COBURN. My, but I've missed you. This is my little sweetheart.

DOTTIE. But, Daddy, you should have given us some warning.

MARGE. We would have had the apartment looking more presentable.

COBURN. Didn't Muriel tell you I was coming?

(They move down. KATE *closes door.)*

DOTTIE. No—we didn't expect you at all. We just had time to get the boys—

KATE. Dottie! Uh—don't you think you ought to introduce us?

DOTTIE. Oh—of course! This is Kate Ault—

KATE. I'm so glad to know you.

COBURN. How do you do?

DOTTIE. *(Moves in* R.*)* And this is Marge Benson. *(Takes hat from* COBURN.*)*

COBURN. Miss Benson—

MARGE. Dottie has said so much about you that we feel we've always known you.

COBURN. *(Flattered)* Well, thank you. Dottie didn't mention that she was living with such charming young ladies.

MARGE. We've been so busy—getting settled. We've only been here a short time.

COBURN. I see—and where are the others?

DOTTIE. *(Pointing to door)* Oh—they went—

MARGE. *(Snatches hat from* DOTTIE*)* What others?

COBURN. I noticed that the name card over your bell downstairs had several more names on it.

MARGE. Oh—that. *(Laughs feebly)* Well, that's very simple to explain. Uh— *(Passes the buck)* Isn't it, Kate? *(Puts hat on bookcase.)*

KATE. Yes, of course! Those are the names of the people who lived here before we moved in.

MARGE. We just didn't think of taking them out. *(Crossing down)* We should have thought of it.

KATE. *(Meaningly)* We certainly should have.

DOTTIE. At least we thought of everything else.

COBURN. I can't understand why Muriel didn't tell you I was coming.

DOTTIE. *(Pulls* COBURN *down* R.*)* She said she had a surprise for me.

COBURN. Well, Dottie, I wouldn't exactly say that you were living in luxury. *(Sits on sofa,* L. *of* DOTTIE.*)*

MARGE. I suppose it does look a little bare.

COBURN. I could easily send you girls some furniture. We have an attic full.

KATE. Oh, no. No. This is just what we want. It gives us plenty of room to rehearse.

COBURN. I see.

MRS. GARNET. *(Running in c.)* Here you are—smelling salts!

COBURN. Smelling salts?

MARGE. Not now, Mrs. Garnet—

COBURN. What's all this?

MRS. GARNET. Oh, are you the doctor?

COBURN. *(Rises)* No, I'm Mr. Coburn—Dottie's father.

MRS. GARNET. *(Pleasantly)* Oh. *(In amazement)* Oh!

MARGE. We were so relieved to find that Mr. Coburn arrived safely—he had no accident at all.

MRS. GARNET. Well, I'm glad to hear that— *(To* COBURN*)* but how is your brother?

COBURN. Well—his rheumatism bothers him from time to time, but—

MRS. GARNET. I know just how he feels. You see, I often get a little pain—right here. *(Indicates back of neck.)*

MARGE. *(Urging her to go)* Of course you do—

MRS. GARNET. In the morning it's almost unbearable—

MARGE. You must tell us all about it—later.

MRS. GARNET. Sometimes I creak. *(Exits L.C.)*

COBURN. Who was that woman?

KATE. That's Mrs. Garnet—our landlady—

COBURN. What did she mean about the doctor and my brother?

KATE. She's had a terrible shock. She hasn't been the same since that accident her brother had.

MARGE. Her brother Stanislavsky.

DOTTIE. Oh—in Oklahoma!

COBURN. Well, that's too bad. *(Sits again at L. of* DOTTIE.*)*

DOTTIE. Daddy, why did you come down to New York?

COBURN. I've come down to see about some publicity Muriel's uncle is arranging for me. I hope that you, Dottie, will be especially nice to Muriel.

KATE. Oh, we'll take care of Muriel.

COBURN. I intend to see some shows and then have an interview with the press Sunday morning.

KATE. Are you going to be here long—in New York?

COBURN. As a matter of fact, I won't be here but a minute—

KATE. That's swell.

COBURN. What?

KATE. For you I mean. I shouldn't think you'd like New York—not after Boston.

COBURN. Well, I suppose I am rather different. I look upon New York as a fascinating place to visit, but I certainly—

COBURN. —wouldn't want to live here—

KATE. *(With him)* —wouldn't want to live here— How true! *(Together)*

COBURN. You see, Muriel's uncle lives out on Long Island, and I'll be staying there. He's quite wealthy—I hope—

DOTTIE. Oh, I thought maybe you'd stay with us for a while.

MARGE. Yes—would you?

COBURN. That's very kind of you, but business before pleasure.

MARGE. Wouldn't you like to see the rest of the apartment? *(Takes COBURN to up L.C.; at his L.)*

COBURN. Yes, I would.

KATE. *(Follows)* Yes—then you won't mind about the rent being raised, will you?

COBURN. Raised?

DOTTIE. Mrs. Garnet said we'd have to raise it somewhere.

COBURN. *(Turns at above chair L.C.)* But I sent you money last month.

KATE. It was her dues she had to pay—Actors' Equity. She's a member now, you know. It was a hundred and nine dollars.

COBURN. Oh—what good does that do her?

KATE. You get a magazine for it.

MARGE. But really, it's a fine organization, Mr. Coburn. You have to belong to be an actress.

COBURN. (*Taking out money*) Well—in that case.

KATE. Equity protects you from the producers. We've been so well protected we haven't been bothered by a producer for months.

COBURN. (*Crossing* R. *to* DOTTIE—*gives her bills*) There you are, and I hope the rent hasn't been made too high.

KATE. No—just high enough.

DOTTIE. You see, we all chip in equal amounts, so dividing it into six parts—

COBURN. (*Laughs loudly. Patting* DOTTIE *indulgently*) Dottie, you never did have a head for mathematics, did you? It should be only *three* parts.

(ALL *laugh.*)

MARGE. (*Crossing in between them. At* COBURN'S L. *Turns him; takes him out*) The kitchen is out this way. (*Pushes* DOTTIE *back.*)

KATE. (*Crossing up, opens door*) And believe me, it *is* a kitchen—a brand new one.

(*Door swings to; bumps* DOTTIE'S *nose. As they* ALL *exit* L.2, *the* C. *door opens and* GEORGE *enters casually. He throws his hat on bookcase, coat on table, then goes to the bathroom, and the sound of WATER running into a tub is heard. (Water effect: small stiff brush on canvas backing.) He comes out carrying his jacket, closing the door. His shirt is unbuttoned, but held closed by tie for quick change. He turns over sign on door*

*so it reads "Performance Going On." Then he
goes to the bedroom R. As he exits, the* OTHERS
return from L.2.)

COBURN. Well, with a fine kitchen like that you'll
never go hungry.

KATE. No. Never. Would you like to see the bedrooms now?

MARGE. I hope they're not all messed up. You see,
in this room— *(Indicating room L.1)* We have three
beds, and in this room—

GEORGE. *(Bellowing from other room)* Where's
my shirt?

(EVERYONE *is startled.)*

COBURN. What was that?

KATE. *(Crossing R. of* COBURN—*starts him* L.*)*
Nothing—probably the radio next door. The walls,
you know—paper thin.

COBURN. It sounded as if it were in the next room.

GEORGE. *(Angry—from bedroom)* No towels in
the bathroom—no clothes anywhere! Is everybody
crazy? *(He enters—dressed in nothing but shoes,
socks and a pair of gaudy shorts)* Who took my
shirt—the blue one? *(Enters; starts to bathroom;
sees* COBURN; *dives behind portiere, holding it over
him.)*

COBURN. *(Crossing up)* Who are you and what
are you doing here?

GEORGE. *(Meekly)* I just came here to take a bath.

COBURN. *(Shouting)* Who is this man?

KATE. *(Crossing R. to* GEORGE*)* I haven't the
faintest idea, but if he knows what's good for him
he'll get out of here—fast!

MARGE. *(Crossing in)* The very idea—breaking
into a strange apartment to take a bath. The very
idea!

DOTTIE. I never heard of such a thing.

GEORGE. I couldn't find my blue shirt.

MARGE. Indeed! And what will Dottie's father think?

GEORGE. Oh! *(In a panic, leaps into his coat.)*

KATE. *(Helps him. Crossing in)* Get out of here. *(Picks up hat)* Is this your hat?

(GEORGE *nods.* KATE *puts his hat on him.)*

GEORGE. Oh, well— *(Tips his hat and calmly starts out)* I have to be running along now.

COBURN. *(Stopping him)* Just a minute, young man. Not so fast.

GEORGE. But I needed a bath and a clean shirt. *(Opens coat)* Look. *(Closes coat quickly; ties belt.)*

COBURN. What made you think you would find them here?

GEORGE. I don't know.

COBURN. How did you get in here in the first place?

GEORGE. I don't know.

COBURN. Perhaps you had a key?

GEORGE. Yes—

COBURN. What?

GEORGE. No, no—no key. *(Crosses down.)*

COBURN. Do you know these girls?

GEORGE. I don't know anything.

COBURN. *(Backing GEORGE toward sofa)* You'll tell me what this is all about, or by Heaven, I'll thrash it out of you.

GEORGE. But I don't know— *(He falls onto sofa)* I'm stupid.

COBURN. *(Pulls him up)* I'll knock some sense into you.

MARGE. *(Crossing to R. of COBURN)* Oh, wait a minute, Mr. Coburn. Don't hurt him. Please stop it.

COBURN. *(Releasing GEORGE and turning to*

MARGE) Perhaps you'll be good enough to explain, then?

MARGE. Well, you see, it's this way— He—

(The C. *door is flung open violently.* TONY *and* NOR-MAN *make it a dramatic entrance, but convincing.* NORMAN *enters first; stands at* L. *on step,* TONY *at his* R. *They wear white jackets.)*

NORMAN. Pardon me, have you seen anything of—

TONY. *(Dramatically)* Ah—we're in time. He hasn't gotten violent yet.

NORMAN. *(Tensely)* Don't do anything to excite that man. He may be dangerous.

COBURN. Who are you?

NORMAN. Bellevue.

TONY. Please step aside—and move—very—slow-ly—very—quietly. *(Cautiously.)*

(COBURN *and* KATE *cross* L.)

COBURN. Good Heavens! The man's—

NORMAN. *(Craftily)* We're your friends. We like you. *(They cross down, careful to keep their backs from the audience)* You remember us, don't you? Come, come, Stanislavsky. (GEORGE *faces front)* We wouldn't hurt you—not for anything in the world.

(The BOYS *grab* GEORGE'S *arms.)*

TONY. *(Breathing a heavy sigh of relief)* Thank God we got here soon enough.

KATE. You said it!

COBURN. Is he—is he—you know—? *(Makes crazy motion at his temple.)*

NORMAN. Absolutely and hopelessly.

TONY. But everything's under control now. I don't think he will cause any more trouble.

GEORGE. *(Starts up)* What's the matter with all of you?

NORMAN. *(Pushes him down)* There, there, little man—don't worry.

COBURN. I had no idea. He barged in here and start d to take a bath.

TONY. Completely nuts.

COBURN. Then he began screaming for clothes—a blue shirt he wanted.

NORMAN. He has a peculiar delusion that he's a laundry man.

COBURN. Oh!

GEORGE. Are you trying to say I'm crazy?

COBURN. Of course you are. You're as crazy as a loon.

GEORGE. *(Jerking away from* TONY *and* NORMAN. *Rises—crossing in)* I am not. I won't have anything like that said about me. I'm as sane as you are. *(Approaches* COBURN*)* I don't know why you have to say I'm crazy—just because I like blue shirts. *(Confidentially—a wild gleam coming into his eyes)* I love blue shirts. I like to feel them. I like to squeeze the collars—especially when they have nice fat necks in them! *(Laughs crazily.)*

*(*TONY *and* NORMAN *move in swiftly; grab him.* DOTTIE *screams.)*

COBURN. *(Alarmed)* Get him out of here.

NORMAN. Don't worry. He won't hurt anyone now.

TONY. Quiet, quiet, Stanislavsky!

(Together)

*(*GEORGE *stands with his tongue out.)*

COBURN. He might have killed us all. How did he get in here?

NORMAN. We were taking some lunatics over to Bellevue, and this one escaped.

TONY. It will never happen again.

COBURN. I certainly hope not.

GEORGE. Me, too.

(TONY *and* NORMAN *drag him out* C., *and the audience sees for the first time "Coca Cola" is lettered across the backs of the white coats.* COBURN *does not see it.* KATE *closes door.* COBURN *mops his brow, and the* GIRLS *breathe sighs of relief.*)

COBURN. *(Crossing* R.*)* I don't know that this is a safe place for Dottie to be in.

MARGE. *(At head of sofa)* But, Mr. Coburn, nothing like that ever happened before.

COBURN. I don't know. It's not safe.

(DOTTIE *pulls him down onto sofa.*)

KATE. But, Mr. Coburn, such nice people live in this building. Why, Arthur Kenny lives right under us, and he's one of the most important producers in show business.

DOTTIE. If you ever get into one of his shows, it's a whole career all by itself.

MARGE. We're great friends. I'm sure he'll look out for us.

KATE. *(At* COBURN'S R. *shoulder)* And he's fond of Dottie. He could do big things for her.

COBURN. Really?

KATE. There's no telling what he mightn't do.

MARGE. And if Dottie were famous, that would mean additional publicity for you.

COBURN. I'll admit I'd like to see Dottie's name in lights.

KATE. I can just see it now—all in lights— "Arthur Kenny presents Dottie Coburn, daughter of Alfred Coburn, one of Boston's most respected and influential politicians."

COBURN. That ought to interest the Lighting Company. I realize that someone like Arthur Kenny could do a great deal for Dottie. You see, I'm interested in the theater myself.

MARGE. Oh, he's definitely interested in us.

KENNY. *(Offstage)* Water, water—*water!*

COBURN. What's that?

(The C. *door is again flung open violently and MR. KENNY enters. He is middle-aged, with a sharp jaw and a dry, unemotional voice that accompanies an habitual sphinx-like expression. At the moment he has in his eyes a wild look. He wears a wing collar, vest, no coat, red morocco slippers; his shirt sleeves are rolled.)*

KENNY. *(With repressed anger)* Are you trying to drown me?

KATE. *(Hoarsely)* Mr. Kenny!

COBURN. *(Rises; retreats to* R. *of sofa)* Another lunatic! Don't get excited, anybody—everybody. Just take it easy. Let me handle this. *(Crosses in to bookcase.)*

KENNY. There's water all over everything, dripping into my gumbo—and last night—galloping over my head!

COBURN. Sh-h-h! Just pretend the water isn't there. Then it'll go away.

KENNY. *(To* GIRLS*)* Is something wrong with him?

COBURN. With me? No, no—nothing's wrong with

anybody. We're just trying to help you. We're your friends; we like you —

KENNY. I'm not interested in your emotions. Where's the bathroom?

COBURN. *(Alarmed) You* want to take a bath?

KENNY. No—it's overflowing all over my apartment downstairs.

KATE. George left it running! *(She exits hurriedly to bathroom. Closes door.)*

MARGE. We're terribly sorry, Mr. Kenny. A perfectly strange lunatic came in here and turned it on.

KENNY. Well, tell him to turn it off.

COBURN. Mr. Kenny?

MARGE. *(Crossing to* KENNY*)* That noise last night—we were rehearsing.

DOTTIE. *(Crossing to* L. *of* KENNY*)* We've been rehearsing for a month.

MARGE. Wouldn't you like to see our production?

KENNY. My dear young lady, it will give me infinite pleasure not to see it.

MARGE. But, Mr. Kenny, it's your play—

KENNY. No!

KATE. *(Coming in—very sweetly)* Mr. Kenny, we have a play we want you to see.

KENNY. Ha! *(Turns and exits* c.*)*

KATE. Did he laugh or burp?

COBURN. So that was Mr. Kenny.

MARGE. *(Sadly)* Yes.

COBURN. The one who was going to do so much for Dottie?

MARGE. Well—he really does like us.

KATE. He's just shy.

COBURN. Unfortunately, I have to spend the weekend on Long Island. *(Gets hat. Crossing to* c.*)* But on Monday morning, as early as possible, I shall return and take Dottie out of this—this insane asylum.

DOTTIE. *(Crossing up—catches his coat)* But, Daddy—

COBURN. I don't want to hear any more, Dottie. After all, I have a certain position to uphold. I don't know what people would say if they knew what went on here.

MARGE. Mr. Coburn, I can explain—

COBURN. I'm sorry, young lady. I'm late as it is. Goodbye. Dottie, you will be ready to leave with me Monday morning. *(Exits C.)*

(DOTTIE *closes door.* KATE *crosses down* L. *to radiator.* DOTTIE *crosses to* L.C. *chair.)*

DOTTIE. *(Pause)* I've got a hundred and nine dollars. You could almost catch up on the rent.

MARGE. What's the use?

DOTTIE. You could all stay a little longer.

MARGE. What are you going to do?

DOTTIE. *(Above chair* L.C.*)* Go back to Boston, I guess.

MARGE. What do you do in Boston? *(Turns; moves* R.*)*   *(WARN Curtain.)*

DOTTIE. Nothing. At least we go to the theater. We see *all* the shows— Daddy's on the Board of Censors.

KATE. I'll bet he doesn't miss a trick.

(NORMAN *and* TONY *enter* C., *carrying the trunk.)*

NORMAN. All clear? What did Mr. Kenny want?

KATE. *(Rises)* Mr. Kenny's mad. He won't see our play.

TONY. Didn't you ask him?

NORMAN. Why didn't you lock him in?

TONY. What did he say?

DOTTIE. He's taking me away Monday.

NORMAN. You mean for good?

DOTTIE. I won't go. I won't. I hate Boston. *(Sits chair* L.*)* It's very depressing.

MARGE. No Dottie, no home, no Kenny. What are we going to do?

(The lid of the trunk flies up and GEORGE *steps out.)*

GEORGE. I know what I'm going to do. *(Running to bathroom)* I'm going to take a bath.

CURTAIN

ACT TWO

SCENE: *The sofa has been turned so that the head is toward up Center. The table is overturned below sofa. One gilt chair is at Right of bathroom door with the phone upon it. The other is up Left Center. The trunk is pushed against the wall down Left. There is a blanket on the sofa. The pipe-holder and goldfish bowl are on the floor down Center. On the bookcase are the lamp and owl, play book, catsup, and alarm clock. The clock, set at 9.00, faces Left so as not to be seen by audience. The bench has been removed.*

It is evening. The wall brackets and lamp are lighted. The bedroom doors are open.

AT RISE: NORMAN *stands up Center holding the skull and a cigarette.* GEORGE *is draped over the chair up Left Center with a knife "in his back."* MARGE *is sprawled on the sofa with a knife "in her tummy."* DOTTIE *is hanging over the table with a knife "in her neck."* KATE *lies on the floor Center with a knife "in her chest."* NORMAN *watches a moment and then flicks his cigarette ashes into the skull.*

NORMAN. *(Using a voice unlike his own)* Strange —they're all dead. This completely wrecks my supposition that the sinister butler was the criminal, as

58

obviously he died before the Crystal Gazer did. It couldn't have been she, because she was killed at the same time the two mysterious sisters met death. Yet the frightened girl was dead when I arrived. *(Puts skull on sofa)* That leaves only the nervous young man and myself. I wonder if— *(He flings open the door* R., *staggering back in horror as* TONY *topples into the room, a fake knife sticking into his chest.* NORMAN *feels briefly for a pulse, then straightens up in terror)* The nervous young man—he's no longer nervous! He's dead—stabbed through the heart. Then—good heavens—that means—of course. —I should have known it from the beginning. The bloody cap in my suitcase—that was the clue. I should have known. I walked in my sleep! Curtain! *(He holds the pose for a moment, then relaxes as the* OTHERS *start getting up from the floor.)*

TONY. Swell!

DOTTIE. Lovely, Norman! *(Sits on sofa.)*

*(*NORMAN *picks up the table and puts it below chair up* L.C.*)*

TONY. *(Looking at alarm clock on bookcase)* The last act was just thirty-one minutes. *(Removes knife, hangs it on hat rack, crosses and sits on radiator* L.*)*

*(*KATE *picks up props; carries them up to chair.* GEORGE *and* KATE *put daggers up* L. *corner.)*

GEORGE. If only Mr. Kenney had seen that performance.

MARGE. *(Removing knife from* DOTTIE'S *neck, puts them in lower shelf bookcase; sits on sofa)* Listen, Norman, we ought to have a corpse for that opening scene. That cushion is just silly.

NORMAN. Well, what can you suggest? You can't double it, and you can't cut it out.

(GEORGE *sits on floor down* C.)

DOTTIE. When Mr. Kenney sees us, he'll just have to use his imagination.

KATE. *(Sits on* R. *edge of table)* A producer—with imagination?

NORMAN. If you did it my way, we wouldn't need a corpse.

GEORGE. *(Sits on floor* C.) What's your way?

NORMAN. Stanislavsky said—

OTHERS. Improvise! *(They stare at him in disgust.)*

NORMAN. It's just because you don't know good theater when you see it.

MARGE. *(Kneels on sofa)* It seems perfectly silly to ruin our whole show by not having a real corpse.

NORMAN. That reminds me, Marge. When you see the body, give a loud scream so I can hear it outside.

MARGE. I didn't want to disturb Mr. Kenney.

NORMAN. Oh—well, all right. But the same thing goes for all of you. *Give* a little more. This is a burlesque of a satirical murder mystery—not a Sunday-school pageant.

GEORGE. Yes. Lawd—

DOTTIE. *(Rises, crossing in to* NORMAN) I think Norman's absolutely right, and I'll bet Mr. Kenney will think so, too.

KATE. *If* we can ever get him up here.

TONY. *(At* L. *of radiator* L.) What's he doing, anyway?

GEORGE. I saw him once—over there. *(Indicates radiator* R.) He still had on that apron. The trouble is he keeps moving around. He won't stay in focus.

(MARGE *crosses* L.)

NORMAN. *(Going to radiator* R.*)* Can't anybody think of a recipe that might calm him?

KATE. I know how to make a Micky Finn.

NORMAN. I said calm him—not embalm him.

KATE. It doesn't hurt you. Just knocks you out.

MARGE. I'm sure he'd love that.

KATE. *(To* GEORGE*)* You *would* have to take a bath.

GEORGE. *(Rising)* How did I know what would happen?

MARGE. We've got to get him up here some way.

GEORGE. I could take another bath.

TONY. *(At radiator* L.*)* He isn't down here.

NORMAN. *(At radiator* R.*)* I can't see him either. Maybe he's in the kitchen.

(GEORGE *goes to* L. *radiator.* TONY *gives way.)*

KATE. Probably whipping up a little fudge.

MARGE. I should think if we told him how vital it was, he'd come up and watch the play. I don't see how he could refuse.

NORMAN. Anything doing yet?

GEORGE. No—I wish I could see more of the room. *(He lies flat on the floor.* KENNEY *appears in the open doorway* C. *and stands watching)* Oh, Mr. Kenny—please come into the room. (KENNY *looks perplexed, then steps into the room)* Dear Mr. Kenny, you little rat—come out, come out, wherever you're at.

KENNY. Well—what do you want?

GEORGE. What do you think?

MARGE. George!

GEORGE. *(Turns and sees who it is—jumps up in confusion)* Oh!

NORMAN. Don't mind him, Mr. Kenny. It's a game he plays.

KENNY. I see.

KATE. We were just hoping you might come up.

MARGE. We wanted to apologize about this morning.

DOTTIE. *(Crossing up* L.C. *to* KENNEY*)* And the noise last night—we were rehearsing.

KENNY. Yes, yes—but that isn't exactly what I came up about.

NORMAN. We were rehearsing "Mostly Murder," the show you produced.

DOTTIE. It must be awfully good—it's still running on Broadway, you know.

NORMAN. He knows that, Dottie.

TONY. *(Crossing in above table)* Of course we haven't had the advantage of your direction—the Kenny touches.

KATE. *(Follows in—laughing)* Your production was a scream. Honestly, when the butler was tortured by the villain, I thought I'd split.

KENNY. *(Dryly)* That's very kind of you.

GEORGE. *(Crossing to* C. *below table)* Oh, no, Mr. Kenny—we mean it.

(ALL *ad lib., backing* KENNY *down* R., *head of sofa.*)

MARGE. *(Follows* GEORGE*)* We were wondering whether you wouldn't come up and see our performance.

KENNY. I'll make a note of it. Now what I really—

TONY. We think you could help us—

KENNY. Yes—some other time. You see, I'm in the midst of a culinary experiment downstairs, and I seem to have run out of flour, so I wondered—well, could you spare a little flour?

DOTTIE. *(Offering flower from her buttonhole)* Here's a little flower.

(NORMAN *pushes* DOTTIE *down onto sofa.* GEORGE *goes to* R. *of* NORMAN.)

MARGE. Dottie!

NORMAN. We do have some. I remember taking some flour out of the coffee tin and putting it in the sugar can.

KENNY. I'd be glad to pay for it.

NORMAN. We had intended using it, but of course, Mr. Kenny—

KATE. Since it's you—

MARGE. To show you how much we think of you—

NORMAN. We'll lend it to you—on one condition.

KENNY. What's that?

NORMAN. That you come up and see our play.

KENNY. Oh, yes—you phone my office and—

NORMAN. Tonight.

MARGE. *(Crossing in)* You've got to see it, Mr. Kenny. You owe it to yourself and to the theater. How do you expect to develop young actors if you won't give them a chance?

KENNY. Now see here—I do use young actors. I make it a practice to encourage unknowns.

DOTTIE. *(Rises)* Couldn't you practise on us—to-night?

(NORMAN *pushes her down.*)

TONY. It'll only take a little of your time, and it might mean our whole careers.

KENNY. It seems to me I've heard all this before. Why don't you see me at my office? *(Turns* L. *to leave.)*

KATE. *(Stopping* KENNY*)* How? "Mr. Kenny's

away. Mr. Kenny's in China." That's all we ever hear in your office. And if we did get in, the first thing you would ask is, "What have I seen you in?" and then, "How can I use you if I haven't seen you?"

KENNY. I appreciate all that—

MARGE. Then you'll do it?

TONY. As soon as you've finished your—your whatever it is?

KENNY. Gumbo Z'herbes—that's what I'm making.

GEORGE. What do you say, Mr. Kenny?

KENNY. Well—

DOTTIE. What's that—that Gumbo Z'herbes? (NORMAN *touches her. To* NORMAN) Well, I never heard of it.

KATE. Dottie, it doesn't make any difference.

KENNY. *(Crossing down to* DOTTIE) You never heard of Gumbo Z'herbes? I thought everyone knew—

NORMAN. Of course, Mr. Kenny—everyone knows. Now, about tonight—

KENNY. It's one of New Orleans' most famous dishes. Most people think it originated in the Congo jungle region, but I have a secret theory that it was really perfected by the Cherokee or Choctaw Indian tribes.

NORMAN. Is that so?

DOTTIE. Is it in Fanny Farmer?

KENNY. *(Pause. Showing complete scorn)* No.

MARGE. Mr. Kenny, why don't you write a cook book?

KENNY. As a matter of fact, I'm preparing one now.

GEORGE. We'll certainly want to use it.

KENNY. It gives you over a hundred different ways of serving pheasant.

KATE. Just what we need.

KENNY. Pheasant is one of the finest of all—
DOTTIE. *(Rises)* Haven't you something on the stove?

(NORMAN pushes her down onto sofa. TONY gives her a look. NORMAN goes up to step. GEORGE goes up behind NORMAN.)

KENNY. *(Crossing to c. door)* Oh, yes, of course.
NORMAN. *(Stopping him)* What about our play? We'd like you to see it tonight.
KENNY. *(In doorway)* No—no—I'm afraid that's quite impossible.
MARGE. We could talk over some more of those intriguing recipes.
KENNY. Well—
KATE. I know one that's a knockout.
KENNY. *(Returning)* That sounds interesting.
MARGE. And you could tell us more about your cook book.
GEORGE. Don't forget the flour.
KENNY. *(Pause)* Well. Perhaps **I could give** you a little time this evening.

(ALL ad lib.)

MARGE. Gosh, Mr. Kenny, you're swell!
NORMAN. *(Running off L.)* I'll get you the flour.
GEORGE. You won't be sorry, Mr. Kenny.
TONY. Our set isn't very elaborate.
DOTTIE. And we haven't all the props. I wish you had some imagination.
KATE. Dottie!
DOTTIE. Well, you said he—
KATE. I was only joking.
NORMAN. *(Running in with can of flour)* Will this be enough, Mr. Kenny?
KENNY. *(Taking it)* Oh, yes—plenty, thank you.

MARGE. Maybe you'll let us taste the gumbo when it's finished?

KENNY. *(Steps down)* Oh, would you?

DOTTIE. We'd love to.

GEORGE. I would love to especially.

KENNY. *(Starting out)* Well, I'll go down and put my gumbo on to simmer. It simmers for two hours.

NORMAN. *(Stopping him)* Two hours?

KENNY. Yes.

NORMAN. We can do the whole show in two hours.

TONY. Do you have much to prepare now?

KENNY. *(Gradually working back c.)* Oh, no. I've already fixed the savories and green and herbes. All I have to do now is make the cream sauce for the shrimp. That won't take a minute.

MARGE. Good.

NORMAN. *(Tries to take him up)* Then you'll be right back?

KENNY. As a matter of fact, I'm trying something new this time—leaving out the leeks, and using fennel and celeriac instead. It might make all the difference. You never can tell.

GEORGE. You never can tell.

NORMAN. *(Turns him up. Trying to get him out)* Well—hurry back.

KENNY. *(Returning. Working back to c. again)* Actually the most important thing is to chop the greens in a wooden bowl. Whatever you do, don't use a meat grinder; chop, chop, chop into little pieces. Then you put the chopped greens back into their boiled juices, and as they simmer—not too hot, mind you— (GEORGE *shakes head)* the tempting aroma assails your nostrils until you can hardly stand it.

GEORGE. I can hardly stand it now.

KENNY. It's worth the trouble, believe me. Crisp, tasty shrimp—fried to a delicate golden brown! Ah—! *(He exhales.)*

(GEORGE *exhales.* KENNY *looks at* GEORGE.)

MARGE. I'm sure it's delicious.
KENNY. Properly cooked, there's nothing like it. Well, I'll be right back. I want to get that recipe. *(He exits* C.*)*

(MARGE *crosses* L. *to* TONY. NORMAN *closes door and crosses down* R. *to* DOTTIE.*)*

NORMAN. In two hours we can do the whole show.
MARGE. Tony, Tony—he's going to see us!

(The OTHERS *ad lib. joyfully.)*

KENNY. *(Sticking his head back in doorway)* Sometimes you use duck instead of shrimps! *(He exits.)*
GEORGE. God bless his gumbo.
TONY. *(Above of table)* Are you sure he's a producer—a theatrical producer? He sounded like a nut to me.
KATE. Well, look at Orson Welles.
DOTTIE. I hope he likes us and nothing goes wrong.
NORMAN. What could go wrong?
MARGE. I wish we had a corpse for that first scene.
NORMAN. Well, we haven't. Now, look—I don't know how long it takes to put shrimp in gumbo, but I vote we get ready.
KATE. *(Going off* L. 1) It takes me longest. *(Closes door after her.)*
TONY. Can't I wear just what I have on?
NORMAN. Yes, but George needs a uniform, and, Dottie, you ought to have on a dress—something long.

DOTTIE. *(Going off to bathroom)* I have just the thing.

NORMAN. Marge, you'd better help her.

TONY. No, I want to run over her lines with her.

NORMAN. All right. Come on, George.

(NORMAN and GEORGE exit R. MARGE looks off L. TONY looks off R. They close in to kitchen door.)

MARGE. Tony—you'll be good tonight, won't you?

TONY. I'll do my darndest, and so will you. Maybe he can use us both.

MARGE. I don't care about myself. I just want you to get something out of it.

TONY. Honey, if he likes me—and if he offers me a job, we can tell the kids about us, can't we?

MARGE. Darling, we can find a nice high housetop to shout it from.

TONY. Marge, I love you so much. I want to be able to give you a present.

MARGE. I know, darling. You will be able to some day. This might be the turning point tonight.

TONY. Yeah, this might be *it!*

MARGE. And, Tony— *(Moves down)* even if it isn't—if nothing happens—

(DOTTIE appears from the bathroom trying to hook up her dress. NORMAN comes out R. and they stand watching in surprise.)

TONY. Marge, I swear I'll take care of you.

MARGE. I know you will.

TONY. You're not to worry—no matter what?

MARGE. I won't, darling—I won't.

(TONY starts to kiss her. They see NORMAN. MARGE and TONY jump apart with obvious embarrassment.)

NORMAN. So—you wanted to go over her lines, huh?

TONY. *(Crossing in)* Now, listen—

NORMAN. It's a fine thing—in a respectable house like this.

MARGE. Norman, there's nothing wrong. Tony and I love each other—

TONY. And what's more—

MARGE. Tony! Is there any objection?

DOTTIE. *(Crossing)* How long have you been that way—you know, the way you are?

MARGE. Ever since last summer.

DOTTIE. Well, why didn't you tell us?

TONY. Because we're—none of your business.

DOTTIE. *(Crossing down R. along sofa)* Goodness, you don't have to bite my head off.

MARGE. He didn't mean to, Dottie—but we've been under a strain.

NORMAN. *(Crossing down C.)* Never mind. We'll talk about it later. Right now we have a show to do. You go in and get ready. (TONY *crosses* R.) And try to forget all that *stuff* tonight. (MARGE *and* TONY *exit to bedrooms* L.1 *and* R. NORMAN *starts hooking up* DOTTIE'S *dress.* DOTTIE *goes up, watching* TONY *off)* I was afraid this would happen.

DOTTIE. What is there to be afraid of?

NORMAN. They haven't time for anything like that.

DOTTIE. It doesn't take long.

NORMAN. How can they act when their heads are full of—of junk?

DOTTIE. Belasco said it makes you a better actress to be in love.

NORMAN. Stanislavsky said—well, you wouldn't understand what he said.

DOTTIE. I think you're just afraid it's going to happen to you.

NORMAN. Don't worry. *(Goes* L.; *pulls out trunk.)*

DOTTIE. But I am worried. *(Sits on trunk)* You know, it could happen, and you might not know it until too late.

NORMAN. *(Crossing to sofa)* What are you talking about? *(Turns sofa. Puts skull onto bookcase.)*

DOTTIE. *(Crossing up* C., *following* NORMAN *around sofa)* In so many plays, they don't find out they're in love until after she's married somebody else, and then they live a tragic life until they're old and gray when they realize their mistake. *(Sits on sofa.)*

NORMAN. What mistake?

DOTTIE. Well, I'm going away Monday, and I don't want to wait until I'm old and gray.

NORMAN. Dottie—

DOTTIE. And that's why I've told you all this, so you'd understand. After all, it isn't easy for a girl to—well, what I mean is if I weren't leaving Monday, I wouldn't—but since I am—well, that's why I thought you ought to know, and I'm glad I told you!

NORMAN. *(Kneeling before her)* Look, Dottie—concentrate. Now—in very simple words, what are you trying to say?

DOTTIE. You won't be mad?

NORMAN. No, Dottie.

DOTTIE. I love you, Norman.

NORMAN. That's fine— *(Pause—slowly realizes what she has said—rising)* Wait a minute, Dottie—think what you're saying—

DOTTIE. I just wanted you to know.

NORMAN. Now, look, Dottie—you're a sweet kid, and—and I like you, but—

DOTTIE. But what?

NORMAN. You have to get that out of your head.

DOTTIE. Why?

NORMAN. Why? Well—damn it, I don't know why. You just have to.

DOTTIE. But. Norman—

NORMAN. It doesn't make sense.

DOTTIE. You don't have to love me. I don't care. Just so you're not angry with me.

NORMAN. I'm not angry at anybody. It's just—it's all wrong. When you want to get some place, you can't let yourself be sidetracked. You have to keep driving ahead, and— *(Sits—takes* DOTTIE's *hand— convincingly)* Look, Dottie, even if I *were* in love with you, can't you see it's not right? Actors can't afford to get married.

DOTTIE. But I love you. That makes it right.

NORMAN. You're thinking with your emotions. You don't realize—

*(*TONY *enters* R. *carrying cap.* TONY *watches him suspiciously.* NORMAN *reacts with embarrassment.)*

TONY. Going over Dottie's lines? I wonder what's keeping Mr. Kenny? *(Puts on cap.)*

NORMAN. *(Carrying props to table)* I don't know, but why don't we run through the opening again? It won't hurt any.

*(*TONY *gets chair from room* R.; *puts it down* R. *for "Mostly Murder.")*

DOTTIE. *(Rises—crossing down* R.) I certainly could stand it.

NORMAN. *(Calling to bedroom)* George—Kate! Marge! Snap it up. We're ready to start.

KATE. *(Off* L.) Be right there.

MARGE. *(Enters wearing hat)* Do you like this?

NORMAN. Yeah, swell!

*(*GEORGE *enters* R. *in makeup and costume of an extremely sinister butler; wears dicky and vest, no sleeves.* NORMAN *helps him into coat.)*

GEORGE. *(In sepulchral tones)* Is everybody happy?

(KATE runs on L.I in makeup and costume of a weird, haggard fortune-teller.)

KATE. Wait'll I fix my scarf.

NORMAN. O.K.! Places—and let's make it good. *(They take places for opening of "Mostly Murder." KATE, seated at table—GEORGE standing. It is a seance with KATE as the medium. NORMAN goes out C. entrance, then sticks his head back in)* Everything all set?

TONY. Wait a minute. You forgot the corpse. *(He picks up cushion and puts it on sofa, covering it with a blanket. He stands behind MARGE, who sits in chair down R.)*

MARGE. Every time I see that thing, I want to laugh instead of scream.

NORMAN. There's nothing we can do about it. O.K.? Let's go. Places— Curtain! *(He exits, closing door behind him.)*

KATE. *(Using queer, metallic voice)* The spirit says—the girl who saw the murder must rise— *(MARGE gets tremblingly to her feet)* She must walk to the bed—and she must pull away the blanket.

DOTTIE. *(Whimpering)* No, no—don't!

(MARGE goes to sofa, pulls away blanket. Her eyes open wide, and she gives a feeble scream, falling to her knees. DOTTIE comforts her. NORMAN rushes into the room.)

NORMAN. Don't anyone move! *(Closes door. To GEORGE)* Who are you? *(Pantomimes removing gloves, "gives" them to GEORGE.)*

GEORGE. I'm the Sinister Butler. *(Puts "gloves" on bookcase.)*

NORMAN. *(He goes to MARGE and bends over her)*

This poor child—why did she scream? *(Picks her up—in his own natural voice)* Damn it, Marge—you can't be laughing.

(TONY sits and ALL except NORMAN start laughing.)

MARGE. *(Laughing helplessly)* I can't help it. It's that cushion—that pillow—and it's supposed to be my dear, dead sister. It's so funny.

TONY. I think it's funny, too.

GEORGE. *(Pulling knife out of pillow)* It does take a lot of imagination. Every time I pull the knife out, feathers blow up at me. And I have to look at that and say the business about blood, blood all around.

NORMAN. Now listen, if anything like that happens when Mr. Kenny is here, we can't break up like this.

MARGE. I'm sorry, but that pillow!

NORMAN. We'd just have to improvise.

MARGE. Stanislavsky—

NORMAN. Yes, Stanislavsky! I'm telling you right now, if anything goes wrong with our show tonight, I'm going to improvise— Why, good Lord, this is our big chance!

KATE. Well, can't you think of anybody we could get in a hurry?

DOTTIE. Maybe Mr. Kenny would be the corpse?

NORMAN. *(Crossing down L.)* Where can we find a corpse at this time of night?

KATE. We ought to have one—a female—

(There is a KNOCK at the door C. TONY rises.)

KATE. It's Mr. Kenny.

NORMAN. *(To GEORGE)* Let him in, will you?

(GEORGE opens door and ushers MURIEL into the room. They all get the same idea, and MURIEL

is frightened by the intent stare. DOTTIE *rises.*
GEORGE *shuts door—crosses down* L. *of* MU-
RIEL.)

GEORGE. *(Not realizing that he still has the knife)*
Muriel—how would you like to be a corpse?
    MURIEL. *(Scared)* No, no—I didn't do anything.

(ALL *close in.*)

GEORGE. *(Waving the knife under her nose)*
You're going to be a corpse whether you like it or
not.
    MURIEL. No. No, I didn't tell him anything—
really I didn't. He doesn't know about your living
together.
    NORMAN. Who doesn't know?
    MURIEL. Mr. Coburn—I didn't tell him.
    KATE. But you were going to.
    MURIEL. No, I wasn't. I meant to tell Dottie he
was coming, but I forgot, that's all—I forgot.
    DOTTIE. Did he say anything about me?
    MURIEL. No—no, he didn't. He went to a show
with my uncle, so you can see he isn't worried.
    MARGE. *(Puts* MURIEL'S *hat, bag, onto bookcase)*
Muriel—darling—we want you to do us a favor.

(GEORGE *at* MURIEL'S L.—MARGE *at* MURIEL'S R.—
they bring her down.)

TONY. And it'll be fun for you.
    DOTTIE. You just have to be dead.
    MURIEL. No, I don't want to.

(GEORGE *gives* R.)

NORMAN. *(Coming in)* You don't understand,
Muriel. We're offering you an opportunity most

girls would jump at. We want you to play a part in our show.

MURIEL. What sort of a part?

NORMAN. It's a grand part—the kind you can get your teeth into. It's the most important part in the play. Why, without you, there wouldn't be any play.

MURIEL. Is it long?

NORMAN. You're on stage almost the entire time.

MURIEL. Oh—I don't know if I could learn all those speeches.

NORMAN. Ah, but that's the beauty of this part—it's all in pantomime. You don't have to say a word.

MURIEL. *(Disappointed)* I don't say anything?

NORMAN. But pantomime is the highest form of acting.

MURIEL. It is?

NORMAN. What do you say, Muriel?

TONY. Come on—be a pal.

MURIEL. *(Doubtfully)* Well—all right.

(TONY *goes* L.; *gets his fake knife off hatrack.*)

NORMAN. Fine! *(Pushing her toward sofa)* Now at the opening, you're lying on that sofa—dead.

MURIEL. Oh, but you said it was a big part.

GEORGE. *(With real knife)* It's tremendous. Just stick this knife in your heart and lie down.

MURIEL. Take it away.

(GEORGE *puts knife on bookcase.*)

TONY. This won't hurt you, Muriel— This is a trick knife. *(He fastens it onto her chest.)*

GEORGE. There—see?

MURIEL. *(Staring down at it in horrible fascination)* Is *that* how they do it?

MARGE. You'll be grand in the part—simply grand.

NORMAN. *(Turns to* MARGE*)* Marge, listen, when you see her, scream as though you meant it. That's my only cue to enter.

MARGE. Don't worry. You'll hear it this time. *(Goes above sofa, crosses down to chair and sits.)*

GEORGE. *(Laying her down)* This is where you are dead, my pet—awful dead, but very, very expressively dead.

MURIEL. Do I just lie here?

GEORGE. That's right.

MURIEL. Can I breathe?

GEORGE. I'm afraid so.

*(*MURIEL *lies down, and* TONY *covers her with the blanket.)*

NORMAN. All right. Let's go.—Places! *(He opens* C. *door to go out, but instead* KENNY *comes in.)*

KENNY. Is everything ready? I'd like to get back to my gumbo very shortly.

NORMAN. Yes, sir, Mr. Kenny, everything's ready. *(Escorts him to trunk* L.*)* Here you are, sir. Lucky to get this seat. Every other one is taken.

KENNY. Thank you.

*(*KATE *fixes trunk; closes door.)*

NORMAN. We'd like you to know that we appreciate your coming up here—even if you tell us afterwards that you didn't like it.

KENNY. You can tell me that when it's over.

NORMAN. I thought I'd better get it in now. I may not feel like it later. *(Going back to* OTHERS. KENNY *looks at his watch)* Everything ready? Don't forget. This is it! Make it good—places!—Curtain. *(He scoots off* C.*)*

(The following action is the same as in the rehearsal before.)

KATE. The spirit says—the girl who saw the murder must rise—she must walk to the bed, and she must pull away the blanket.

DOTTIE. No, no—don't!

(MARGE *pulls away the blanket, revealing* MURIEL. *Then she screams—a frightening, piercing scream.* NORMAN *rushes into the room, but before he can speak,* MURIEL *sits up.*)

MURIEL. Is anything the matter? Are you all right?

NORMAN. Oh—no—no!

MARGE. Muriel, you're supposed to be dead!

MURIEL. Oh, but I thought you—I thought you were hurt.

GEORGE. You're not supposed to think—you're dead!

MURIEL. (*Getting up angrily*) Well, I don't see anything to get excited about. After all, I've never practiced the part.

TONY. She wants a rehearsal to play a corpse.

NORMAN. (*Running over to* KENNY) I'm terribly sorry, Mr. Kenny.

KENNY. All right—all right! Let's get on with it.

KATE. Can we begin over again?

MURIEL. (*Still angry*) Well, if I have to lie here, I want something to drink. I'm thirsty!

KATE. You're thirsty?

MURIEL. Yes, I am.

TONY. Look—we'd better use the pillow.

KATE. No—wait a minute, Tony. Of course she's thirsty. (*To* MURIEL—*sweetly, but with a fiendish gleam in her eye*) I'll get you a nice, refreshing drink. (*She dashes out* L.2.)

NORMAN. (*To* KENNY, *after watching* KATE *off*) Mr. Kenny, if you'll just bear with us for one more minute, then we'll go right through it.

KENNY. What have you done with the second act?

NORMAN. What do you mean?

KENNY. Well—some people seem to think the scene between the butler and the Crystal Gazer was too gruesome—too horrible.

NORMAN. But that's the punch to the play.

KENNY. Yes, I know. Frankly, I had hoped that scene would have tremendous box office appeal, but no one knew it was supposed to be funny.

NORMAN. We plug it for all it's worth— *(Goes up to table for manuscript.)*

KENNY. We'll see.

KATE. *(Coming in with drink in colored glass—crosses to* MURIEL*)* Here you are, Muriel darling—special for you.

MURIEL. *(Takes it—suspiciously)* I hope it isn't alcoholic.

KATE. No— It's a surprise. I know you'll like it. Drink it down.

MURIEL. *(After draining the glass—with a pleased smile)* That's very good. Thank you. Now we can begin.

(NORMAN, *who has been watching, now turns his attention to* KENNY. MURIEL *gives glass to* KATE. KATE *gives glass to* GEORGE. GEORGE *puts glass on bookcase—returns.)*

KATE. *(Watching her anxiously)* How do you feel?

MURIEL. All right.

KATE. Don't you feel dizzy?

MURIEL. Certainly not.

KATE. *(Turns to* GEORGE*)* What a girl!

(During the above, MURIEL'S *smile fades and she falls back onto sofa.* TONY *catches her.)*

DOTTIE. What have you done to her?

KATE. Won't hurt her a bit.

TONY. Micky Finn?

KATE. In person.

MARGE. Kate, you're a genius.

KATE. Think nothing of it. I'll do the same for you some day.

MARGE. No, thank you. Kate, she even looks dead.

GEORGE. I'd hate to wake up and find it in bed with me. Blood, blood all around. *(He takes catsup from bookcase and smears some on* MURIEL'S *front)* There—now you know what a fishcake feels like. *(He pulls the blanket up over* MURIEL.)

NORMAN. *(Crossing up, puts script on table— crossing)* Is Muriel satisfied?

KATE. We're all satisfied.

NORMAN. Well, let's go, then. Places! Ready, Mr. Kenny?

KENNY. Quite.

NORMAN. Places! *(Steps out* C. *door)* Curtain!

(Once again the same procedure is carried out.)

KATE. The spirit says—the girl who saw the murder must rise. She must walk to the bed, and she must pull away the blanket.

DOTTIE. No, no—don't!

(MARGE pulls away the blanket, revealing MURIEL, then she gives a terrifying scream. The door opens, and NORMAN rushes into the room. Right behind him is MRS. GARNET.)

MRS. GARNET. *(Running in)* What happened? Good heavens!

NORMAN. Oh, for the love of— *(Slams door.)*

Mrs. Garnet. *(Crossing down C.)* Oh—it's Mr. Kenny.

Kenny. See here. *(To Others—annoyed)* This is ridiculous. When you're ready to give your performance, let me know. *(Starts to leave.)*

(All *ad lib.*)

Norman. *(Stopping him)* Wait a minute, Mr. Kenny. There won't be any more interruptions.

Kenny. Well—hurry up with it. *(Goes back to trunk.)*

Tony. We were doing a play, Mrs. Garnet.

Mrs. Garnet. *(Crossing in to sofa)* A play? But that scream?

Marge. That's part of the plot. I have to scream.

Mrs. Garnet. Oh, I know—you were just acting. Well, I don't mean to presume, but could I watch it?

Kate. Yes, yes—anything!

Marge. Only, hurry, Mrs. Garnet, please. Mr. Kenny's getting impatient.

(Kenny *winds his watch.*)

Tony. Look, Mrs. Garnet—you keep telling him how much you like us—as actors, I mean. We might all get jobs out of it.

Mrs. Garnet. I certainly will. My, that would be fine.

Tony. Don't forget now.

Mrs. Garnet. No, no, I won't.

(Norman *assists her. She crosses and sits on trunk up of* Kenny.)

Norman. Mrs. Garnet, won't you sit over there, please?

Mrs. Garnet. Yes, thank you very kindly.

NORMAN. All right, let's go. Places again. Come on, kids, and don't let all this disturb you. Everybody ready? *(Starts up.)*

MRS. GARNET. Yes, indeed. *(To KENNY)* They're such attractive youngsters, aren't they?

KENNY. Why—I suppose so.

MRS. GARNET. And such fine actors! Aren't you enjoying the play?

KENNY. Well—

MRS. GARNET. Oh, I think it's wonderful—so entertaining. Too sweet for words.

TONY. Please, Mrs. Garnet—not yet.

MRS. GARNET. Oh--excuse me. Go right ahead.

NORMAN. *(Weakly, as he exits)* Curtain!

(The same procedure is repeated—this time a little grimly.)

KATE. The spirit says—the girl who saw the murder must rise—she must walk to the bed, and she must pull away the blanket.

DOTTIE. No, no—don't!

(MARGE pulls away blanket, revealing MURIEL. She gives her loud scream and falls to the floor. MARGE repeats her scream, all the KIDS become uneasy. Finally MARGE gets up and screams hoarsely right at the C. door. The door opens, and NORMAN enters, struggling to get away from two POLICEMEN.)

NORMAN. Let me go! Let me go, you fool!

1ST COP. Don't anyone move!

(GEORGE stands at head of sofa. DOTTIE stands beside him next MARGE. TONY sits on foot of sofa. Together they shield MURIEL's covered body

from Cops. Mrs. Garnet *rises.* Norman *starts
to leave.)*

2ND Cop. *(To* Norman*)* Where do you think
you're going? Get back over there. Go on.
  Kenny. *(Rises)* Next time it'll be the Marines.
(To L *of* Mrs. Garnet.*)*
  1st Cop. All right now—who screamed?
  Marge. I did, Officer, you're making an awful
mistake— *(Her voice is lost in the ad lib. protests of
the* Others.*)*
  1st Cop. One at a time! One at a time!
  Kenny. See here, Officer, you have no right to
come breaking in here.
  1st Cop. We got a call to investigate—
  Kenny. That is the young lady who screamed,
but there was nothing wrong.
  Dottie. No, she screamed when she saw the body.
  1st Cop. Body? What body?
  Marge. *(Has instinctively covered* Muriel*)* She's
mistaken. There isn't any body.
  George. What would we be doing with a corpse?
  1st Cop. *(Eyeing* George's *weird makeup)* Who
are you?

(2ND Cop *crosses to table; picks up owl; shows it to*
1st Cop.)

George. I'm the sinister butler—I mean, I live
here.
  1st Cop. *(Indicating props on table)* What's all
this paraphernalia?
  Kate. It's mine. It's all part of our show.
  Dottie. *(Steps out)* We're a crime ring, that's all.
  Kate. We were just having a little fun.
  2ND Cop. What kind of fun do you suppose these
people have?
  1st Cop. *(To* Kate*)* You live here, too?

KATE. Yes.

TONY. Look, Officer—

NORMAN. I live here, too. We all do. This is "Mostly Murder" and— *(Moves above table.)*

2ND COP. Murder?

TONY. *(Rises; sits)* Yes, it's running on Broadway now.

KENNY. I staged it.

2ND COP. Oh, the brains of the gang, huh?

1ST COP. Listen, all I want to find out is why did you scream?

MARGE. Because I had to. I can explain—

1ST COP. What are you trying to hide?

MARGE. Nothing, Officer.

KENNY. *(Crossing in—firmly)* Once and for all, Officer—there has been no crime.

1ST COP. It sounds very suspicious to me. Have you any means of identification? *(Crosses in.)*

KENNY. *(Crossing in)* Certainly. Mrs. Garnet— she's the landlady—she can tell you who we are. *(2ND COP moves in down R.C. MRS. GARNET doesn't speak but tries to see beyond KENNY. He turns to her)* Mrs. Garnet—tell them we live here. *(She doesn't speak)* Mrs. Garnet—please!

MRS. GARNET. You mean—really?

KENNY. Of course, really.

MRS. GARNET. *(Rises)* Oh, is the play over? *(Hesitantly begins to sit again.)*

KENNY. These policemen think we're up to something.

MRS. GARNET. *(Crossing)* Oh—I thought they were in it too. *(Goes C. between COPS. KENNY goes L.)* Oh, you missed it. You should have been here. It was just wonderful. I loved it. It's a shame it's so short. The most exciting part was when she saw the murdered girl lying there—

1ST COP. Murdered girl? Where?

KENNY. Mrs. Garnet, please. *(At below trunk.)*

MRS. GARNET. *(Hesitantly)* Why, right there under that blanket.

1ST COP. All right, all of you—line up against that wall.

(ALL *cross* L.)

2ND COP. *(Pushing* MRS. GARNET *over* L.*)* You, too—and no monkey business. *(He draws a revolver.)*

1ST COP. You won't need that, Joe. (2ND COP *puts revolver away.* MRS. GARNET, *bewildered, returns to trunk and sits)* If this is a joke—

(They go to sofa and pull away blanket. MURIEL *is lying there with knife sticking in her chest. The* COPS *reverently remove their caps for a moment.)*

2ND COP. Felonious assault. I better call Headquarters.

1ST. COP. Wait a minute, Joe. I'm not so sure—

2ND COP. With a knife sticking in her heart, you ain't sure?

NORMAN. *(Crossing in)* But, Officer—

(DOTTIE *follows to table.)*

1ST COP. According to regulations I have to warn you that anything you say can be used in evidence against you.

NORMAN. This is the end— Why does it have to happen to me? *(Sits on table.)*

2ND COP. They always crack up when they see the victim.

NORMAN. She's not dead!

2ND COP. She ain't denying it, is she?

1ST COP. Don't be so hasty, Joe. Appearances can be deceiving.

2ND COP. Don't that knife mean anything to anybody?

KENNY. *(Crossing to c. to 2ND COP)* This has gone far enough. Officer, my name is Arthur Kenny. I'm a theatrical producer. It's perfectly simple to explain this whole ridiculous mess. It's all make-believe—a show—a play.

2ND COP. You mean like a fantasy?

KENNY. Exactly! These people are all actors.

1ST COP. Oh—actors!

KENNY. So they believe.

1ST COP. Say, that looks like— *(Pulls up knife)* I thought so.

2ND COP. Lemme see. *(Tastes catsup)* Catsup. Is it a fake?

1ST COP. Yes, we often use that in the Police shows. *(Goes above sofa to KENNY)* We—we seem to have made a mistake.

KENNY. Yes, indeed you have.

2ND COP. *(Tugs on 1ST COP's sleeve)* Ain't anybody dead?

1ST COP. It was a misunderstanding, Joe. I'm sorry we disturbed you.

2ND COP. Yeah—we're both sorry.

KENNY. I ought to report you to your superiors.

1ST COP. *(Starts up)* Well—we'll be going now.

NORMAN. *(Crossing up c.—opens door)* Don't let us hurry you.

KENNY. Anyone with a modicum of intelligence would realize that this girl is only pretending— *(Goes to MURIEL.)*

2ND COP. Yeah—sure. So long, folks.

KENNY. *(To MURIEL)* Here, you—get up.

(ALL ad lib. "Goodbye.")

1ST Cop. Good night, everybody!

KENNY. *(Shakes her)* I said get up—the play's over. (MURIEL *doesn't budge. Going up to door)* Wait a minute, Officer! There *is* something wrong here! This girl's unconscious.

2ND Cop. Maybe she's only tired.

KENNY. I can't make her move.

1ST Cop. *(Crossing down R. of sofa)* So—I was right all along. *(Examines* MURIEL's *eye)* She's been drugged.

KENNY. Drugged? *(Turns to* KIDS) This is preposterous. I refuse to be mixed up in anything like this. *(Starts to go.)*

NORMAN. *(Closes door)* No, Mr. Kenny—don't go.

2ND Cop. *(Pushes* KENNY) You ain't going nowhere. Get back over there.

KENNY. But I tell you I had nothing to do with it.

2ND Cop. *(Pushes* KENNY) Go on.

1ST Cop. *(At R. of sofa)* No one's leaving here until we know more about this.

KENNY. I've a good mind to call a policeman.

2ND Cop. Right here, Mister.

NORMAN. You're not going to let anyone leave— anyone at all?

1ST Cop. *(Crossing up C.)* No, it's against the law to drug people. Why did you do it?

GEORGE. *(To* NORMAN) There's no use stalling any more. You better confess, Stanislavsky!

NORMAN. *(Getting his "cue")* Yeah, yeah. Gimme a break, Officer. I'll talk. I done it. I poisoned her.

MARGE. Norman, stop it. You'll only get us into trouble.

1ST Cop. Be quiet, young lady. *(To* 2ND Cop) Write this all down—I'll go slowly. *(To* NORMAN) Why? What made you do it?

NORMAN. I was covering up my tracks. She had

the goods on me. She was gonna squeal, so I knocked her out.

2ND COP. Yeah? What did she know?

1ST COP. *(To 2ND COP)* I'll ask him. *(To NOR-MAN)* What did she know?

NORMAN. She was a stool pigeon. She knew about the Black Shirt gang.

2ND COP. This is a case for the G-man.

NORMAN. And she knew about the Red Flannel Boys.

2ND COP. *(Taps 1ST COP's arm)* Say—that's for the Dies Committee.

NORMAN. So I gave her the works. But I couldn't help it, I tell you, I couldn't help it. He made me do it. I had to—*see?* I stood it as long as I could. Now I can't take it any more. You got to protect me, or he'll rub me out. He won't stop at nothin'! Don't let him get me, don't let him.

1ST COP. We better take them all in. Call the wagon, Joe.

2ND COP. Yeah— *(Crossing down L. to sofa)* I better get an ambulance, too.

NORMAN. *(Step down)* Wait a minute, Officer. You can't take us to jail.

KENNY. I protest. I haven't time.

2ND COP. Naw—we just gonna drive you around to see the city. *(Goes to phone.)*

NORMAN. Don't touch that phone! If you do, the building will be blown into a thousand pieces, and you with it!

1ST COP. Get away from it, Joe. *(Going R. toward 2ND COP)* He may not be kidding!

KENNY. *(Crossing in)* Officer, I'll phone the police for you.

NORMAN. *(Leaps in front of him)* Don't let him. Can't you see he's trying to commit suicide? He wants to take the easiest way out. *(Backs away down L.)*

(The Cops *follow* Norman *in to* c. Muriel *shows signs of coming to.)*

1st Cop. *(They move in)* How do you disconnect that bomb?

(Muriel *moves hand.)*

Norman. *(Pause. Seeing* Muriel *and stalling for time)* I'll tell you—I'll tell everything. But first let me get this crime off my conscience. It's driving me crazy.

1st Cop. Is this a confession?

Norman. Yes—I'll even sign it—anything to relieve my tortured mind.

1st Cop. Take it down, Joe. Go ahead.

(Muriel *moves.)*

Norman. *(Watching* Muriel—*speaking the italicized words loudly directly at her, deliberately trying to make her sick)* I never liked her. I couldn't stand her. She made me *feel sick?* (Muriel *sits up painfully)* I could see nothing but *blood, blood, blood, all over the place.* (Muriel *rises)* I said to myself, *how would you like some soft scrambled eggs and warm beer curdling up in your stomach?* (Muriel *quietly stumbles toward the bathroom. At the door she stops and listens some more—looking very ill)* I began to see strange things. One time in Boston *I saw a girl run over by a steam roller, and she was squashed flat, and her insides spread out all over the street!*

(Muriel's *hand flies to her mouth. Dizzily, she turns and dashes into the bathroom, slamming the door behind her.)*

2ND Cop. *(Turning around)* What was that?

GEORGE. Don't worry—the place is haunted.

MRS. GARNET. *(Rises—pointing to bathroom)* I don't understand. I thought she was supposed to—

TONY. *(Crossing down—stops her)* Mrs. Garnet—wait until the play is over—remember?

MRS. GARNET. Oh! Are you beginning again?

KATE. And how—

KENNY. *(Intervening)* See here, Officer. This is absurd. I can't waste my time like this. Furthermore, I have a gumbo downstairs—

2ND Cop. Don't make me laugh! You ain't got no gunboat downstairs.

KENNY. No, no—gumbo— Gumbo Z'herbes, a shrimp dish—all the different savories and greens and herbes—all chopped up in a wooden bowl into little pieces. (COPS *exchange looks)* Little teensy, weensy pieces—

2ND Cop. Are you wacky?

KENNY. No, I'm cooky—I mean, I'm cooking. There's nothing wrong in that, is there? And there's nothing wrong in anything going on here either.

1ST Cop. I suppose there's nothing wrong with this girl over here?

NORMAN. *(Quietly)* What girl?

1ST Cop. The one with the knife— *(Crosses down R. of sofa—stops as he sees MURIEL isn't there)* What's going on here?

2ND Cop. Hey! It ain't right stealing corpses.

1ST Cop. *(To NORMAN)* What did you do with her?

NORMAN. *(Meekly)* I chopped her up into little teensy, weensy pieces in a wooden bowl. *(Moves L.)*

2ND Cop. Yeah! You're all under arrest. We'll sweat it out of you.

(They advance L.)

DOTTIE. Ladies don't sweat—they glow.

2ND COP. *(Takes handcuffs out)* Cut out them wisecracks. We'll take you into Headquarters—all of you. *(There is a NOISE at the bathroom door— and* MURIEL *staggers out—slams door. The* COPS *wheel)* Geez—it's her. She's walking.

1ST COP. *(Crossing to sofa)* Who are you?

MURIEL. *(In hollow tone—crossing to sofa)* I'm dead.

2ND COP. *(Crossing down* C.*)* How does it feel?

MURIEL. Awful. *(She flops onto sofa.)*

KENNY. I hope you are satisfied now that the young lady has not been poisoned.

2ND COP. She just said she was dead.

KENNY. Undoubtedly she was mistaken.

1ST COP. *(At head of sofa—after examining* MU-RIEL *briefly)* She seems to be asleep.

KENNY. Well, I only wish that my productions could attract audiences the way yours does. And now, if you don't mind, I'll get out of here.

(ALL *ad lib.*)

NORMAN. Mr. Kenny—

MARGE. Please don't be angry.

DOTTIE. It wasn't our fault.

NORMAN. No, no—stop him. Stop him! *(Grasps* KENNY's *lapels; turns him to* L.*)* No, I ain't gonna take the rap for you. I'll come clean this time.

KENNY. *(Throws* NORMAN's *hands off)* I warn you, young man—

2ND COP. Is there a crime, or ain't there?

NORMAN. *(Retreats onto step)* I'll say there is, and it's big, too—bigger'n you think. It'll make heroes out of you guys. Just give us a break and we'll re-enact the whole thing for you, so you can see how it was planned. Only don't let that man say nothing. He'll try to stop us, but don't let him. You gotta listen—what d'you say?

1st Cop. All right, I'll take a chance. Joe, you cover the door and don't let anybody in or out.

(WARN Curtain.)

2nd Cop. O.K., Mac! *(Goes up* R. *of* C. *door.)*

1st Cop. *(Advancing)* Come on, you. *(Pushes* Kenny, *who mumbles—over to sit above* Mrs. Garnet) Sit down, and don't make any disturbance, hear?

Norman. O.K. The rest of these people were sitting around—like this. *(They quickly assume places for "Mostly Murder."* George *and* Dottie *cover* Muriel) —like this.

Kenny. *(Grimly—to* Mrs. Garnet) Well, how do you like the play?

Mrs. Garnet. *(After a pause)* It's a little confusing.

Kenny. I agree.

Mrs. Garnet. I like a clear plot like the Marx Brothers always have. I saw—

1st Cop. *(Standing ominously close to* Kenny) Quiet, Madame!

(The 2nd Cop *stands beside the door.)*

Norman. *(Opening door)* Now this is how it was. I was right outside the door, and she was in a trance —like that. Curtain! *(Ducks off stage as before—)*

*(*2nd Cop *grabs his wrist. The same procedure is followed.)*

Kate. *(Rapidly—afraid of interruption)* The spirit says—the girl who saw the murder must rise —she must walk to the bed, and she must pull away the blanket.

Dottie. No, no—don't!

(MARGE *goes to the bed, pulls away the blanket and screams loudly. The* KIDS *turn expectantly to the doorway.* NORMAN *rushes in; holds the pose.*)

NORMAN. Don't anyone move.
KENNY. *(Dryly)* Good—you made it!

(NORMAN *drops his pose and looks dejectedly at* KENNY.*)

BLACKOUT

CURTAIN

ACT THREE

SCENE: *The furniture is back approximately as it was in Act I. A clothesline has been strung across the arch. On it hang* MURIEL'S *skirt, coat. At Right is another line on which hangs a pair of pajamas and a pair of stockings. At Right on the step are a cup and saucer and a glass of water. The phone books are piled on the step at the Left. There is a cigar on the bookcase and newspapers on the floor below the sofa.*

It is morning. Sunlight streams through the open bedroom door at Left.

AT RISE: TONY *sits on the chair down Right with his feet on the radiator and reading the drama section.* GEORGE *lies on the sofa with his eyes closed.* NORMAN *sits in the gilt chair, Left Center, reading the book section, and* DOTTIE *lies on the trunk, reading the funnies which are spread on the floor.* MARGE *is pacing.* ALL *are in pajamas and robes.*

There is a silence for a moment and then NORMAN *kneels at Left radiator and looks down the hole.*

MARGE. Any sign of him yet?

NORMAN. Nope, quiet as a churchyard.

GEORGE. Anybody going to church this morning? *(They* ALL *stare at him)* I just wondered.

(KATE, *also in pajamas, comes from the bathroom
and throws a pair of wet silk stockings to*
GEORGE.)

KATE. Here, hang these up, will you? *(Exits back
to bathroom.)*

TONY. *(Reading)* Three shows closed last night.
(DOTTIE *giggles)* What's so funny about that?

DOTTIE. Peter Rabbit's in the worst mess.

TONY. Yeah, but *he'll* get out of it.

GEORGE. *(Hanging stockings over line down* R.*)*
That girl has the longest legs.

NORMAN. Where do you suppose Kenny's gone?

GEORGE. *(Lies down)* Maybe he's dead. Last night
was enough to kill anybody.

MARGE. *(Genuinely upset)* Why don't we forget
about last night!

TONY. At least he explained things to the cops and
then stayed to see the rest of the show.

KATE. *(Comes from bathroom carrying wash-
board, Lux and throws slip to* GEORGE; *closes bathroom door)* Here—work on that. *(Exits* L.2.*)*

GEORGE. *(Holding it up gingerly)* So now I take
in washing! *(A KNOCK at the door.* GEORGE *leans
over slip—eagerly)* Come in. (MRS. GARNET *enters*
C.*)* Oh—it's you. *(He goes* R.; *hangs slip on end line
down* R.*)*

MRS. GARNET. Doing your laundry?

MARGE. What is it, Mrs. Garnet?

MRS. GARNET. *(Crossing down* L.*)* Well, I hate to
keep insisting, but—

NORMAN. *(Rises—crossing up* R.*)* Don't tell me. I
have it—the rent!

MRS. GARNET. *(Pleased)* Oh, you have it?

NORMAN. We have part of it, anyway— Dottie—

(DOTTIE *rises—exits* L.1.*)*

MARGE. Did you like the play last night, Mrs. Garnet?

MRS. GARNET. The first part I didn't understand so well—

GEORGE. No, we didn't either.

MRS. GARNET. But the rest was fine—just fine.

TONY. Ah, a rave notice.

MRS. GARNET. Did Mr. Kenny like it?

(Enter DOTTIE *with money.)*

MARGE. We don't know. He hasn't even been near us.

DOTTIE. *(Giving* MRS. GARNET *money)* Here—this helps some, doesn't it?

MRS. GARNET. Well, it catches you up on the last two months, but what about this month?

GEORGE. *(At bookcase)* You see—appeasement is no good.

MRS. GARNET. At least—now I won't have to keep your furniture (KATE *enters)* when you leave, thank goodness.

KATE. What do you mean? We're not leaving.

MRS. GARNET. It's either you or the lady upstairs. She don't like policemen. They make her nervous.

NORMAN. *(Rises)* Look, Mrs. Garnet, we'll have the money for you. Dottie's father is going to take care of that.

MRS. GARNET. That's fine. *(Goes up* C.)

DOTTIE. *(Rises—moves in to* NORMAN) Norman, I'm not sure Daddy—

NORMAN. There—you see, Dottie guarantees it.

MRS. GARNET. Well, if I don't get it, I'll have to give you immediate notice.

MARGE. How long can you wait?

MRS. GARNET. Until tomorrow.

GEORGE. Blitzkrieg!

MRS. GARNET. Yes, there's somebody else wants

the apartment. *(Going to* C. *door)* Well—have a nice breakfast. *(Exits.)*

*(*NORMAN *sits trunk.* DOTTIE *sits chair* L.C. MARGE goes down* R. *to* TONY. GEORGE *moves* L.; *sits on steps.)*

KATE. Nice breakfast! *(At up* L.*)*

(They ALL *sit glumly. The bathroom door opens, and* MURIEL *staggers out. She has on a pair of pajamas and bathrobe ten sizes too large for her— a wet towel around her head.)*

MURIEL. *(Hanging up her blouse with stain in it)* The catsup won't come out.

DOTTIE. How do you feel, Muriel?

MURIEL. I feel like a jigsaw puzzle that hasn't been put together.

GEORGE. Maybe there are some pieces missing.

MURIEL. No, I'm all here. When I was in the bathtub I looked.

DOTTIE. Why did you get in the bathtub with your clothes on?

MURIEL. I was leaning over it, and I must have had a dizzy spell. It was almost as though somebody had pushed me.

*(*KATE *dusts off her hands, moves in down* C., *most pleased with herself.)*

NORMAN. I think you ought to stay here several days, Muriel—take a nice long rest.

MURIEL. *(Sadly)* I want to go home.

TONY. Go ahead.

GEORGE. You'd make quite a hit at Grand Central.

MURIEL. Just as soon as my clothes dry out, I'm

going home, and I'm going to tell Mr. Coburn just what happened.

MARGE. Muriel, you wouldn't do that—

KATE. *(Grimly)* Would you?

MURIEL. *(Crossing R.)* Oh, I better go. I wish I had a toothbrush. *(She staggers off to bathroom.)*

(KATE *goes L. to radiator.*)

GEORGE. Maybe her clothes won't dry very fast. *(He gets a glass of water from the step and sprinkles it on the clothes.)*

MARGE. Dottie, do you think she'll really tell your father?

DOTTIE. No. She's just sensitive.

MARGE. Can't you make your father change his mind?

NORMAN. Yeah, you've got to stay here.

DOTTIE. *(Pleased)* Oh, Norman—

NORMAN. Or we get thrown out tomorrow.

DOTTIE. *(Disappointed. Rises. Goes up)* Oh—the money.

MARGE. It's not just that, Dottie, but we know how much you love the theatre.

GEORGE. It's too bad.

DOTTIE. Oh, stop feeling sorry for me, all of you! You're the ones to be sorry for—walking from office to office and getting more and more discouraged. I'm glad I'm getting out of it. I'm glad—glad! *(An embarrassed pause)* Don't you believe me?

NORMAN. Not good enough, Dottie.

DOTTIE. I'm glad I'm getting out of it. I'm— *(She looks inquiringly at them—then weakly)* I *am* glad, I tell you. I like Boston. It's quiet and restful and—and horrible. *(Sits on pile of phone books; weeps.)*

NORMAN. *(Rises—crossing up C. to R. of DOTTIE)* Dottie—please—

DOTTIE. Leave me alone. I hate you.

KATE. Is there anything else that could happen?

MARGE. *(Upset)* Yes. Yes, there is. Everything's all wrong, and we're—you might as well know now. Tony and I are married.

(A moment of stunned surprise.)

NORMAN. Married?

GEORGE. No kidding?

KATE. Legally?

TONY. Yes, and permanently, too.

DOTTIE. How wonderful.

NORMAN. When did all this happen?

MARGE. Last August—when our play opened.

NORMAN. You should have told us.

KATE. Sure, you should have.

DOTTIE. Just think—married!

NORMAN. Gosh, that's—that's marvelous.

GEORGE. Well, congratulations! We ought to celebrate.

NORMAN. You bet. Married! Wow! *(Takes cigar from bookcase—offers it to* TONY*)* Have a cigar.

TONY. Say, I'm the one who's married—not you.

NORMAN. Don't be so stingy. We can help celebrate, can't we?

GEORGE. Maybe some day we can be godfathers.

DOTTIE. And me—can I be a godmother?

MARGE. Of course you can—all of you.

KATE. We'll stick together—that's the important thing.

MARGE. You're all crazy but I love every one of you.

*(*KENNY *knocks at the door and enters; gets tangled in laundry.)*

DOTTIE. *(Running over to him)* Mr. Kenny! I'm going to be a godmother!

KENNY. *(Steps down)* You are?

DOTTIE. It's all right—we're married.

KENNY. All of you?

DOTTIE. No, Marge and Tony.

KENNY. Congratulations!

GEORGE. Mr. Kenny—

NORMAN. I guess you didn't think much of our show last night— } *(Together)*

TONY. The way you rushed off afterwards—

KENNY. Oh—it wasn't the show. It was my gumbo. You see I had hoped to perfect it before the Escoffieres' dinner next week. But I guess it's just no use.

DOTTIE. Cheer up, Mr. Kenny. Things are never as dark as they seem.

KENNY. You should have seen my gumbo! *(Goes down toward chair.)*

MARGE. *(Crossing in)* That's a shame.

KATE. But. Mr. Kenny—what about our show?

(ALL *ad lib.*)

TONY. *(Crossing in with MARGE)* Yeah—do you think you could use us—any of us?

KENNY. Well — considering the handicap you were working under—your show was good. Even the business in the second act made sense.

GEORGE. You mean the horror scene with me and Kate?

KENNY. Yes, yes. That was all right. But the most convincing acting you did—and this is what sold me on you as a group—was that improvision scene you staged with the policemen before the show started.

NORMAN. Stanislavsky! There! What'd I tell you!

MARGE. Be quiet, Norman.

KATE. *(To KENNY)* Yes?

KENNY. *(Crossing down* L. *of chair* L.C.*)* So this

morning I went to have a talk with my business manager. I thought it might pay to put out a road company of "Mostly Murder," using all of you.

(Enter MURIEL *from bathroom.)*

MARGE. How wonderful!

KENNY. Well— *(He breaks off as* MURIEL *staggers into the room. She goes over and very carefully feels her clothes, then returns to the bathroom.* GEORGE *gets his glass of water and starts sprinkling the clothes again.)*

NORMAN. What'd your business manager say?

KENNY. He—uh—he said— *(*KENNY *is fascinated by what* GEORGE *is doing.)*

GEORGE. I'm just trying to shrink them down to fit her.

TONY. What did your manager say?

KENNY. He thought I was out of my mind. *(Staring at* GEORGE*)* Well, maybe I am. *(Back to* KIDS*)* Yes, it would be box-office suicide to send a show on the road with no names in it. *(Sits.)*

[MARGE *goes in.* GEORGE *goes* R.; *sits foot sofa.)*

NORMAN. *(Pause)* No—naturally not.

KATE. This has been the shortest run of my entire career!

KENNY. It's a clever show and you're clever actors. Perhaps if it had some tremendous publicity build-up—

TONY. You wouldn't be doing another play, would you?

KENNY. No, not until next Fall.

TONY. Next Fall— *(Goes up to* MARGE.*)*

DOTTIE. That's something, anyway.

KATE. You'll be in Boston.

DOTTIE. Oh, Golly— I never have any fun!

KENNY. *(Rises)* Well—I'm sorry. I really am. *(Crosses to* C.*)* I—I'd better get back to my kitchen such as it is—now.

NORMAN. It's not your fault, Mr. Kenny. You've done everything you could.

GEORGE. Your kitchen?

KENNY. Yes. My flooded kitchen. I want to try my gumbo again.

GEORGE. *(Rises—crossing to* KENNY*)* Look, Mr. Kenny—because you've been so swell to us, we'd like to do you a favor. How would you like to make your gumbo in *our* kitchen?

KENNY. What for?

GEORGE. Well, my bath messed your kitchen all up and besides maybe it'll change your luck.

KENNY. Yes. It might make a difference.

GEORGE. *(Holding his stomach)* I know it would.

KENNY. Fine—I'll run right down and get all the things I need.

GEORGE. We'll all help you bring it up. There might be a lot to carry— *(Hopefully)* Mightn't there? *(Motions* NORMAN *and* TONY *to follow* KENNY. *They exit* C.*)*

KENNY. *(As he exits)* Yes, there's quite a bit.

GEORGE. Maybe tomorrow you'd like to try a steak— *(To* KATE*)* a nice thick steak? We'll be right back. *(He exits* C., *leaving door open.)*

KATE. *(Sits on trunk above* DOTTIE*)* Well, at least we *eat* today.

MARGE. What are we going to do about Mr. Coburn tomorrow morning?

KATE. Dottie, think hard. Isn't there anything we can do for him so he'll let you stay?

MARGE. We can't wait for Mr. Kenny to do something next Fall—

KATE. No matter how you look at it, it comes right back to the same thing—Dottie. She's got to stay!

MARGE. Listen, when Muriel gets through telling what she knows, we won't have a prayer of keeping Dottie.

KATE. Is it against the law to strangle people?

MARGE. Couldn't we make a big play for Mr. Coburn—flatter him?

KATE. That pompous, stuffed shirt!

MARGE. Kate, he's Dottie's father.

KATE. That's not her fault.

(COBURN *enters* C.)

DOTTIE. He can't help being dumb. *(By way of explanation)* He's a politician.

COBURN. *(Coming down angrily. Slams door behind him)* What's wrong with being a politician?

DOTTIE. Why, Daddy!

KATE. Why, Mr. Coburn! How nice of you to drop in like this.

COBURN. We'll see how nice it is! Where's Muriel?

MARGE. *(Passing the buck)* Muriel?

DOTTIE. *(Ditto)* Muriel?

KATE. Muriel? How should we know?

COBURN. Isn't she here?

KATE. This is the last place in the world Muriel would want to be.

COBURN. She said she was coming here last night, and then she never came home—all night long.

KATE. Well, that's New York for you

DOTTIE. *(Crossing in)* Daddy, you've just got to let me stay here.

MARGE. *(Crossing up* R C. *Holds clothesline up. Trying to make* COBURN *leave)* But we haven't time to discuss it now. We're expecting visitors any minute—I'm afraid.

KATE. *(Crossing in to* COBURN*)* And we have to get dressed, so if you'll excuse us—

COBURN. Well—

MARGE. *(Crossing down)* You'd better hurry. It may be later than you think.

DOTTIE. *(Crossing in)* Yes, any minute now, it may be *too* late.

COBURN. I can't imagine where Muriel spent the night.

(They have crowded him to the door. MURIEL staggers in from the bathroom; feels her clothes. MARGE goes L. to KATE.)

COBURN. *(Crossing up C.)* So! She is here!

MURIEL. *(Indicating her clothes)* They're still wet.

COBURN. Just what's going on here?

KATE. Muriel wasn't feeling very well, and she wanted to be quiet *(To MURIEL)* —very *quiet*.

DOTTIE. Now, Daddy—you mustn't believe your eyes.

MARGE. You see, Mr. Coburn—

COBURN. I'll get to the bottom of this in my own way. Muriel, have you anything to say for yourself?

MURIEL. Yes, I have.

KATE. Muriel!

MURIEL. *(Almost in a trance)* When I first got here, there was a man in a rowboat, and he tried to attack me and make me wear a girdle like a Communist. Then they wanted me to be a corpse, and they poisoned me, and I was unconscious. When I came to, there were twenty policemen in the room, and I bled catsup all over my front, and then they tried to drown me. I don't think they like me. And it's all because I know about Dottie letting everybody move into her apartment.

COBURN. Is that everything?

MURIEL. Gracious, isn't that enough? *(She ends on a triumphant note, and the other GIRLS cringe, but COBURN turns to MURIEL angrily.)*

COBURN. Muriel Foster, you ought to be whipped —spreading malicious falsehoods about Dottie.

MURIEL. But it's all true.

COBURN. It's fantastic nonsense! A man in a row-boat—Communists—twenty policemen! Where are they?

MURIEL. Well—they were all here last night.

COBURN. Have you been drinking?

KATE. (*Crossing in* C.) She got pie-eyed, Mr. Coburn. We were trying to hush it up.

COBURN. It's disgraceful, and now I'm almost late for my appointment with the reporters at my hotel. I might have lost all that important publicity.

MARGE. I'm sorry you were inconvenienced, Mr. Coburn, but hadn't you better hurry now?

COBURN. Well, it wasn't your fault, young lady. (*Looks reproachfully at* MURIEL) Tsk, tsk, tsk.

MURIEL. (*Desperately*) I know there were some men here.

KATE. Imagination is a tricky thing!—Well, hurry along, Mr. Coburn.

COBURN. Yes, I must be going.

(There is a KNOCK on the C. *door.)*

MURIEL. There! There they are—coming back. You'll see.

COBURN. Now we'll find out! Tell them to come in. (*Exits to bathroom, peeks out.*)

KATE. (*Wearily*) Come in. (*The door opens, and* MRS. GARNET *enters*) Mrs. Garnet, you don't know how glad I am to see you.

MRS. GARNET. Thank you. You said Mr. Coburn would take care of—

MARGE. Yes, Mrs. Garnet.

MRS. GARNET. (*Coyly—to* COBURN) You needn't try to hide in there. I see you.

COBURN. I wasn't hiding. (*Slams door.*)

MARGE. Mrs. Garnet, please come back some other time, we're busy now—we're busy rehearsing.

MRS. GARNET. Oh—well, that's fine. I'll call the police.

MARGE. Yes,— No! Mrs. Garnet—

MRS. GARNET. They wanted to see the rest of the show.

MARGE. Yes, but—Mr. Coburn isn't a very experienced actor, and he'd be nervous with an audience.

MRS. GARNET. I see—could I come back later?

MARGE. Whenever you like.

MRS. GARNET. I'll be very quiet. *(She exits.)*

COBURN. *(Enters)* So that poor old woman is your twenty policemen! Really, Muriel. I'm ashamed of you.

MARGE. Mr. Coburn, won't you change your mind about taking Dottie away?

COBURN. Well, perhaps I was hasty. I was unduly excited at the moment.

KATE. I'm pretty excited right now. Don't forget your appointment with the reporters.

COBURN. *(Crossing up c.)* Oh, yes—the reporters.

MARGE. What about Dottie, Mr. Coburn?

COBURN. Well, we'll see about that.

MARGE. It's too bad you're in such a hurry.

COBURN. *(Crossing down c.)* Perhaps I could let them wait another few minutes.

MARGE. Oh, no, Mr. Coburn—no. *(She hurries him to the door, and as they reach it, from the hallway the boys are heard singing, "Hi Diddledee dee." COBURN listens—puzzled.)*

KATE. *(Frantically)* You never did see our bedrooms, did you, Mr. Coburn? (She takes one arm and MARGE the other. KATE trying to go off L. and MARGE off R. COBURN stays in the middle, finally freeing himself in time to see the procession enter GEORGE, NORMAN, TONY and KENNY have formed a* *parade, the boys bearing foodstuffs and pots and pans.* GEORGE *carries a turkey on platter,* TONY *follows carrying two quarts of milk.* NORMAN *carries two copper pans.* KENNY *enters last with large chopping bowl heaped with greens and vegetables. They see* COBURN *and dash for the door.)*

COBURN. *(Stopping them)* Just a minute—just a minute!

MURIEL. *(Crossing up* C. *to* R. *of* COBURN*)* There —I told you so—I told you so. He was the one in the rowboat.

(KENNY *puts bowl on table.)*

COBURN. *(Exploding)* So this is the insane laundry man from Bellevue is it? (GEORGE *retreats to bathroom door—puts platter on bookcase)* And these are the two keepers, are they?

DOTTIE. Now, Daddy, you mustn't get excited.

(NORMAN *puts pans on floor below bookcase.)*

COBURN. *(Yelling)* I'm not excited.

DOTTIE. Then don't shout so. *(Quietly)* You should be very quiet. I'm going to be a mother.

COBURN. What?

DOTTIE. I mean—a godmother—I mean—maybe.

COBURN. Oh—well, I think you're all crazy.

TONY. *(Gives milk bottles to* MURIEL*)* Just a minute. You can't talk to my wife like that.

COBURN. Your wife?

TONY. That's right. Any objections?

COBURN. Why, no—of course not.

TONY. *(Offering cigar he got from* NORMAN*)* Have a cigar. *(Goes* L. *to* MARGE.*)*

COBURN. Thank you. *(Takes it—then throws it down angrily)* I don't want a cigar. All I want is to take my daughter out of this place.

NORMAN. Mr. Coburn, Dottie belongs in New York—in the theatre.

COBURN. The theatre isn't any place for her. The kind of shows they put on nowadays aren't fit to see, much less act in.

NORMAN. You have the wrong slant on it.

COBURN. The wrong slant? Is it wrong for me to disapprove of my daughter living in this apartment? Is that wrong—especially when she isn't so bright?

KENNY. Now see here, Mr. Coburn. These children have been much too busy rehearsing my play, "Mostly Murder," to—

COBURN. "Mostly Murder"? Why, that's the play I saw last night, and I was so incensed at the torture scene in the second act that I left immediately.

KENNY. It's not that bad—worse luck. *(Turns up to bookcase.)*

COBURN. I have no more time to spare. Muriel, take Dottie into her bedroom and help her pack. She's coming with me.

DOTTIE. But, Daddy, I don't want to go.

COBURN. I don't care what you want—you're going!

DOTTIE. Norman—please. Do I have to?

NORMAN. No, you don't have to.

DOTTIE. I don't?

NORMAN. You're eighteen—you're old enough to do what you want to do.

DOTTIE. I am?

COBURN. *(To* NORMAN*)* Why, you little—

NORMAN. And what's more, you can't make her! Besides, *(Desperately)* I love Dottie, see?

DOTTIE. Oh, Norman!

NORMAN. And I want to marry her.

DOTTIE. Norman, do you mean it?

NORMAN. Sure, I mean it. *(He grabs her—kisses her passionately.* DOTTIE *clings to him, and he realizes it's true)* Well, I'll be— I *do* mean it!

COBURN. Are you coming with me, Dottie?

NORMAN. *(Weakly)* No, she isn't.

COBURN. I thought you said she was old enough to speak for herself. Dottie, I'm waiting.

DOTTIE. *(To* NORMAN*)* You weren't just Stanislavskying, were you?

NORMAN. *(Sincerely)* No, Dottie, I meant what I said—I do love you.

DOTTIE. *(To* COBURN*)* Then I won't leave. I'm staying right here where I belong. Norman needs me to look after him.

(MURIEL *goes down; sits on trunk; puts milk bottles on floor.)*

COBURN. *(Crossing down* L. *They retreat)* So you've turned my daughter against me, have you! I thought something like that would happen—living in these surroundings. You ought to be punished some way—all of you. You ought to be arrested for—for stealing her money—for kidnapping Muriel!

(During the above lines, MRS. GARNET *enters* C. *very quietly and sits on piled phone books and watches. She wears a fringed shawl instead of the sweater, has put on long earrings and a brooch at her throat. She thinks she is watching a play and reacts accordingly.)*

NORMAN. Listen, Mr. Coburn—

COBURN. Just how do you intend to support my daughter?

NORMAN. I'll support her by working?

COBURN At what?

NORMAN. At anything. We're—uh— *(Rashly)* we're going on the road in "Mostly Murder."

COBURN. Oh, you are?

KENNY. (To NORMAN) I have something to say about that.

COBURN. You have nothing to say about it. It's a shocking play and that's what I'm going to tell the reporters this morning. (Turns to C.)

KENNY. Mr. Coburn, you don't seem to realize—

COBURN. I'm not on the Board of Censors for nothing. I'll have it banned in Bos on.

KENNY. Now, see here—

COBURN. I'll make radio speeches about it and I'll incorporate it into my coming election campaign. (Turns up; starts to exit.)

KENNY. Wait!—I can't have anything like that. I have a reputation to uphold in New York.

COBURN. You won't have when I get through with you.

KENNY. But why do you want to close my play?

COBURN. Because it's my duty and besides it'll teach Dottie a lesson, and she'll come running home to me fast enough.

KENNY. I had nothing to do with your daughter— or with any of these impossible creatures. Mr. Coburn, be reasonable—

COBURN. I'm sorry, but I must. In the meantime, Muriel—I want you to stay here with Dottie.

MURIEL. (Covers her face; groans) Oh!

COBURN. I'm going to meet the reporters now, and when I get through, everyone in the country will know what sort of a play "Mostly Murder" is.

KENNY. Oh, I don't care about the play. It means nothing to me,—but I do care about my name. I won't have it, I tell you—I won't have my name dragged through a filthy scandal. Oh, I wish I'd never seen any of you. Why, it'll ruin me. (Crossing down) Why, I may even be expelled from the Escoffiers. (Sits foot of sofa.)

COBURN. Too bad! Too bad! (To MRS. GARNET) Oh, how do I get to the Hotel Dixie?

MRS. GARNET. *(Confidentially)* Don't worry—you're very funny. *(Sits again.)*

COBURN. This is the screwiest place I was ever in! *(Exits furiously.)*

(KENNY *rises; goes up* C.)

MARGE. We didn't mean anything like this to happen.

NORMAN. Gosh, Mr. Kenny—I'm sorry.

KENNY. Well! You needn't think you're the only ones who ever heard of Stanislavsky. With the kind of publicity he's going to give me, I could send out ten companies of "Mostly Murder."

(ALL *ad lib. "What?"*)

MARGE. You mean you were only pretending?

NORMAN. It was just a joke?

} *(Together)*

(WARN Curtain.)

KENNY. *(Returns down)* I could use an old set from one of last year's shows—find someone for the corpse—rehearse it and get it up to Boston in a week.

KATE. What do you say, Mr. Kenny?

DOTTIE. Will you?

NORMAN. How about it?

} *(Together)*

KENNY. We go into rehearsal tomorrow!

(The KIDS *ad lib, excitedly.*)

MURIEL. Say—you can't do that.

GEORGE. Uh—oh—it's in again.

MURIEL. *(Crossing* C.) I'm going to go right over to that hotel and tell Mr. Coburn how you fooled him.

KENNY. *(Stops her at his* R. *After a pause)* Young lady, how would you like to be a corpse?

MURIEL. No, I don't want to.

(DOTTIE *sits sofa.* GEORGE *below sofa,* L. *foot on it.)*

NORMAN. *(With great emphasis—then rapidly)* But think of the dramatic value of that! You're lying on the sofa dead. I rush over to you. I stare down at you and in your limpid tragic eyes I read the history of the whole case. In your simple, virtuous posture I see the solution. In your poor, beautiful face there is untold suffering. Your fists are clenched—so! *(Brings his fists up clenched. She does likewise)* And in that last noble gesture there is recorded for posterity the gallant struggle of womankind down through the ages—

MURIEL. *(Completely swept away—eagerly)* It does sound good.

CURTAIN

END OF PLAY

OUT OF THE FRYING PAN

PROPERTY PLOT

ACT ONE—SCENE I

Draperies on door R.
Radiators down R. and I jog.
Bulletin board (clamps, papers, pencil, letter).
Wash line hooks.
Sofa R.C.
Table up R.
Chair up R.
Bench up L.C.
Chair L.C.
Hatrack up L.C.
4 Cushions on steamer trunk.
Phone books L. on step C.
Bookcase up R.C.
Phone on bookcase.
Samuel French playbook on bookcase.
Large old-fashioned trunk down L.
On table up R.:
    Owl.
    Globe.
    Skull humidor.
    Lamp.
    Pipe rack.
    3 Pipes.
    5 Knives and forks.
Foil up L. corner.

Fencing mask on hatrack.
Grey chair off door R.
Suitcase at door L.1.
2 "Y" towels in towel rack in bathroom.
Pots, pans, etc., in kitchen.
Hook, potholders on kitchen door.
Bracks down L. and R.
Knife in pillow head of sofa. This is a large knife
    cut off 3" or 4" from the point; 30" of welding
    wire welded to this cut edge makes a loop to fit
    over head or into skirt, neck or under sweater,
    shape for TONY's or MURIEL's neck. *Remove
    cutting edge from all knives.*

SCENE II

Sofa parallel to footlights.
Phone book under L. end of sofa.
Cup and saucer under R. end of sofa.
Cup and saucer on radiator down R.
Cup and saucer on table.
Dust cloth on sofa.
2 Cushions returned to trunk.
Remove slippers.

ACT TWO

Sofa turned head up L.C.
Table overturned down R. of sofa.
Phone on chair up R.
Blanket on sofa.
Knife in pillow on floor up R.
On Bookcases:
    Alarm clock.
    Catsup.
    Owl.
    Playbook.
    Lamp.

Chair c. to up L.C.
5 Knives as described in Act I.
Globe on floor down R.C.
Pipe rack down R.C.
Trunk against wall up L.
Remove bench.
Bathroom door closed.

ACT THREE

Grey chair down R. faces off.
Bench up L.C.
Phone books on step at L. end.
Cup and saucer (on R. of step).
Glass of water (on R. of step).
Wet pajamas (on line R.)
Wet stockings (on line R.).
Suit coat and skirt (on line C.).
Cigar on bookcase.
Funnies on floor R. of trunk.
Playbook on chair down R.
Magazine section on chair L.C.
Papers below sofa.
Bathroom door closed.
R. Door closed.

PROPERTIES OFF STAGE

Down Left:
    Money (Act III).
    Girdle.
    KATE's mules.
In Kitchen:
    Bread on plate.
    5 Hamburgers, French fries, serving spoon on
        platter.
    5 Plates.
    Catsup.

Dish towel.
2 Aprons.
Sugar can.
Compo glass.
Overshoes.
Bathrobe.
Package hamburger.
Laundry box.
List on box.
Shirts (1 blue) (in laundry box).
Pajamas (in laundry box).
Shorts (in laundry box).
Kitchen towels (in laundry box).
5 Dagger rings as described in Act I.
3 Cups and saucers (on tray).
Dust cloth (on tray).
Pink towel.
Smelling salts.
Cigars.
Glass of water.
Blanket.
Clock.
Off Center:
    2 Quarts of milk.
    2 Copper pans.
    Platter, turkey.
    Bowl, vegetables.
    2 White jackets, plain in front, but "Coca Cola"
        lettered across back.
Off Right:
    Clothes tree for offstage changes.
    Table and mirror.
    Pan of water for GEORGE to wet hair.
    Thumb tacks, pad and pencil.
    Pile of clothes.
    Tuxedo on hanger.
    Blue shirt.
    1 Sock.

      Pajamas.
      Bathrobe.
Off Bathroom:
      Shaving material.
      Face cloth.
      Washboard.
      Lux.
      Clothespins.
      Wet slips.
      Wet stockings.
      Wet stained blouse (duplicate of MURIEL'S blouse, stained red).
      Small brush (water effect).
      Towel for KATE.
      Roll of bills for COBURN.
      Small flower for DOTTIE.
Holster, revolver for 2ND COP.
Cigars.
Cigarettes.

OUT OF THE FRYING PAN

COSTUMES

ACT I—SCENE I—WOMEN

DOTTIE: Navy blue dress. Tan trench coat. Red beret. Blue gloves. Colored striped bag.

MURIEL: Blue suit. Blouse with full jabot. Blue hat, red edging. Blue bag and gloves.

KATE: Beige dress and cape. Brown hat, bag and gloves.

MARGE: Powder blue dress. Blue coat. Kerchief on her head. Brown bag.

MRS. GARNET: Black skirt. Black pumps. Loose-collared blouse. Blue sweater.

SCENE II

DOTTIE: Blue slacks. Blue checked suit with red dicky. Sneakers. Light blue figured dress. Red lacings.

KATE: Grey skirt. Yellow sweater. Blue blazer.

MARGE: Two-piece green linen suit.

ACT TWO

DOTTIE: First Scene dress, long blue with big hooks at back for costume.

KATE: Black lace dinner dress, long sleeves. Black lace scarf on head for costume.

MARGE: Second Scene outfit. Strange black hat for costume.

ACT THREE

DOTTIE: Pink robe. Red-white striped pajamas. Red moccasins.

MURIEL: Man's green-white pajamas. Man's black-white, small check robe. Man's blue, fleece-lined slippers. Small towel wrapped about head.

KATE: Maroon robe. Turquoise blue ascot. Blue mules.

MARGE: Blue velvet robe. Blue slippers.

MRS. GARNET: Fringed shawl. Long earrings. Brooch.

ACT I—SCENE I—MEN

GEORGE: Blue-grey trousers. Blue shirt. Black sleeveless sweater.

NORMAN: Dark grey trousers. Suspenders. White shirt.

TONY: Grey slacks. Undershirt. Overcoat. Scarf. Tan shirt (in laundry box).

SCENE II

GEORGE: Coat to match Scene I trousers. Tie, overcoat, hat, blue-white striped shorts. Black socks and garters.

NORMAN: Bow tie. Coat to match trousers.

TONY: Camel's hair sweater, maroon sweater. Sport jacket.

MR. COBURN: Light grey suit. Blue shirt. Blue tie, blue cornflower, grey hat.

MR. KENNY: Dark grey trousers. Vest. White shirt, rolled sleeves, winged collar, grey ascot. Red morocco slippers. Glasses.

ACT II

GEORGE: Same as Scene I. Tuxedo trousers, vest, coat, white combo collar, shirt front dicky, black bow tie.

NORMAN: Dark grey coat, trousers, white shirt, bow tie.

TONY: Grey slacks. Sport jacket. Tan shirt. Maroon tie. Cap.

MR. KENNY: Dark grey suit. White shirt. Red tie.

MAC and JOE: New York City police uniforms. Holsters and revolvers.

ACT III

GEORGE: Blue pajamas. Brown robe. Black slippers.

NORMAN: Grey pajamas. Brown slippers.

TONY: Tan pajamas. Chocolate robe. Brown slippers.

MR. COBURN: Brown suit. White shirt. Red tie. Grey hat.

MR. KENNY: Dark blue suit. Blue shirt. Red-blue tie.

OUT OF THE FRYING PAN

LIGHT PLOT

10 Front lights, 1000 Watt.
 6 1000 Watt.
 4 400 Watt.
 2 350 Section X-ray.
 5 Strips.
 2 brackets.
   Table lamp.

Portable board.
12 outlets.
 1 to 3000 Watt plates.

Bastard amber.
Pink.
29 Blue.
#3 Straw.

Pono and door bells.
2 Makeup lights off Left and Right.
3 Sections 40 Watt footlights.
1000 Watt spot through door Left.

OUT OF THE FRYING PAN

PUBLICITY THROUGH YOUR LOCAL PAPERS

The Press can be an immense help in giving publicity to your productions. In the belief that the best reviews from the New York and other large papers are always interesting to local audiences, and in order to assist you, we are printing below several excerpts from those reviews.

"To have heard the audience roaring you would have thought that 'Hellzapoppin' had been crossed with 'You Can't Take It With You' and betrothed to 'Charley's Aunt.'"—*New York Times.*

"—a youthful swing to it—"—*New York World-Telegram.*

"—screwball comedy— It kept an appreciative audience laughing almost continuously." — *New York Journal.*

"—a youth and laugh show."—*New York Daily Mirror.*

"One of the surprises of the current theatrical season—one of the merriest Broadway events—an underlying ring of truth that makes it human as well as amusing."—*New York Post.*

"This play by Francis Swann exhibits a nice spontaneity and naturalness, with the result that it is one of the more enjoyable frolics of the season." —*Brooklyn Eagle.*

"—one of those romps through bedlam."—*P.M.*

" 'Out of the Frying Pan' possesses a decidedly appealing quality."—*New York Herald Tribune.*

"—the author has hit the nail on the head—and written a colorful farce."—*Newark Sunday Call.*

"This is a gay and light-hearted comedy."—*Cue.*

"One of the most heart-warming and hilarious plays about the show business ever to create bedlam on both sides of the footlights— A few seconds after the rise of the curtain the laughs start, and are practically continuous until the final curtain falls."—*Billboard.*

"—downright funny—"—*Baltimore Sun.*

"—most hilarious comedy."—*Baltimore News-Post.*

"—genuinely amusing and packed with laughs."—*Washington News.*

" 'Out of the Frying Pan' is good fun, being bright, inventive, and not at all concerned with tiresome probabilities."—*The New Yorker Magazine.*

"—a smash-hit—"—*Evening Capital, Annapolis, Md.*

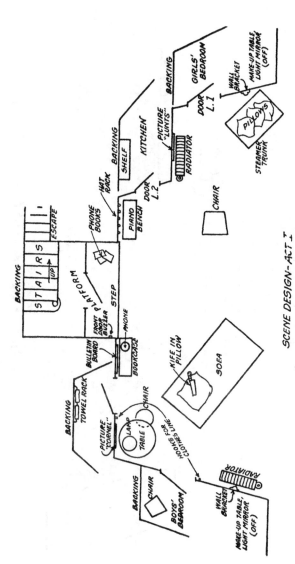

SCENE DESIGN—ACT I
"OUT OF THE FRYING PAN"

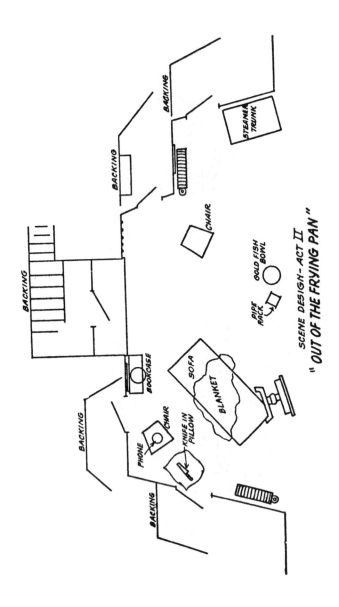

SCENE DESIGN – ACT II
"OUT OF THE FRYING PAN"

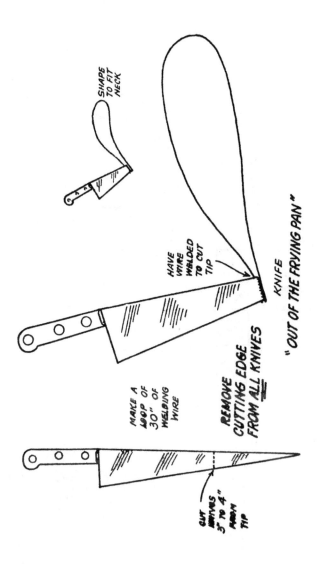

SHAPE TO FIT NECK

HAVE WIRE WELDED TO CUT TIP

KNIFE

MAKE A LOOP OF 30" OF WELDING WIRE

REMOVE CUTTING EDGE FROM ALL KNIVES

CUT BRINGS 3" TO 4" FROM TIP

"OUT OF THE FRYING PAN"

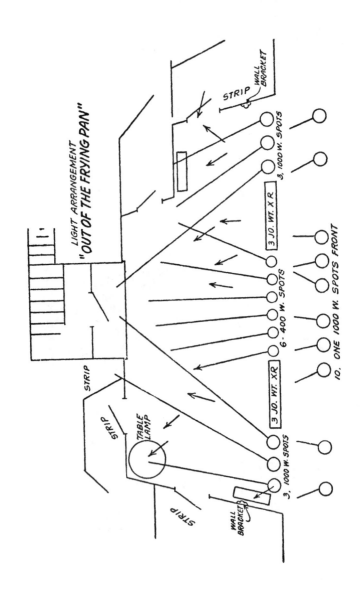

LIGHT ARRANGEMENT
"OUT OF THE FRYING PAN"

STRIP

WALL BRACKET

STRIP

3, 1000 W. SPOTS

3 JO. WT. XR

6 - 400 W. SPOTS

10, ONE 1000 W. SPOTS FRONT

3 JO. WT. XR

STRIP

TABLE LAMP

3, 1000 W. SPOTS

STRIP

WALL BRACKET

CPSIA information can be obtained
at www.ICGtesting.com
Printed in the USA
LVHW082228071019
633432LV00044BA/1713/P

9 780573 613500